Teacher Narratives From the Eikaiwa Classroom: Moving Beyond “McEnglish”

Edited by Daniel Hooper and Natasha Hashimoto

Candlin & Mynard ePublishing
Hong Kong

Published by Candlin & Mynard ePublishing Limited
Unit 1002 Unicorn Trade Centre
127-131 Des Voeux Road Central
Hong Kong

ISBN: 978-988-75194-0-9

Teacher Narratives From the Eikaiwa Classroom: Moving Beyond "McEnglish"

Life and Education in Japan Series

Series Editors: Diane Hawley Nagatomo and Melodie Cook

Candlin & Mynard ePublishing Limited was founded in 2012 and is incorporated as a limited company in Hong Kong (1830010). For further information, please see the website: http://www.candlinandmynard.com

Cover image by Akiyuko by Shutterstock

Contents

Foreword

Ryuko Kubota
University of British Columbia

Eikaiwa (英会話) [English conversation] is a unique Japanese term. Although certain world languages can be abbreviated and represented by *kanji* [Chinese character], such as Chinese (中), French (仏), German (独), and Spanish (西), only English (英) is used in combination with *kaiwa* (会話) [conversation]. This simple fact indicates how eikaiwa is a popular enterprise, sustained by the perceived utility and superiority of English as an international language. Moreover, the world of eikaiwa contains manifold interests, desires, and ideologies with regard to race, language, gender, and economy, shaping the experiences of teachers, learners, and business owners. It also entails multiple relations of power, entangled with privilege, marginality, and inequalities. The world of eikaiwa indeed offers fascinating topics for scholarly investigations from educational, psychological, sociological, and applied linguistic perspectives.

In 2007, I stayed in Hasu (all names are pseudonyms), a mid-sized city in rural Japan, to understand the significance of eikaiwa for Japanese adults learning English in informal contexts. I was initially interested in interviewing and observing learners in corporate-run eikaiwa classes. However, due to difficulties of gaining access, I focused on community-based lessons. Interviews with a number of Japanese women and men of all ages, as well as participant observations, revealed the varied roles that eikaiwa plays in their lives (Kubota, 2011a, 2011b, 2016, 2018). Tae, for example, enjoyed socialising with her classmates in the weekly eikaiwa lesson. While Yayoi unabashedly expressed her dream of marrying a white man, Misaki, who actually married a white American eikaiwa teacher during that year, expressed her surprise and regret for such a desire to be held by other women. She eventually fulfilled her dream to teach English to children but her salary was only half of that of native English-speaking colleagues. For two women, Hiroko and Kiyomi, learning eikaiwa enabled them to escape from their personal struggles. Eikaiwa also offered hope and refuge to Kazuo, a man struggling at work due to a demotion from office duties to assembly work. Conversely, gregarious Daichi simply wanted to broaden his friendship circle through learning English, but eventually he landed a dream job that allowed him to work overseas. Two men at a local manufacturing company were taking an evening English class at their workplace. They expressed their fascination with English and cultures of inner-circle countries, but they had divergent attitudes toward China, a country where their company was expanding business. Other women and men were learning English to raise their TOEIC scores for career advancement.

These portraits reveal the multiple and diverse stories of eikaiwa learners, which are influenced by broader forces, such as language ideologies and various relations of power. Toward the end of my stay in Hasu, it became clear to me that in order to understand the world of eikaiwa more fully, multiple players and structures would need to be examined. In particular, I became interested in the stories of other players, those of eikaiwa teachers. Although teachers were not my research focus, I had opportunities to individually interview two white American male teachers working at one of the eikaiwa companies in the city.

Michael had a bachelor's degree in philosophy and English, whereas Paul had majored in science and communication with a focus on video production. They were the same age—in their late 20s—and had had no previous training in teaching. Michael had been in Japan for 20 months and had also taught at another eikaiwa school in Hasu. Paul had been in Hasu only for 9 months. Both of them displayed a stereotypical image of eikaiwa teachers as world travellers. Michael said "The idea is to keep traveling as long as I can. Not settling but keep traveling." Paul had been burned out from his work in Hollywood and he "really wanted to travel."

However, their interview accounts provided a sense of their concern for education and struggles with ethics as language teaching professionals. Shortly after they started teaching, they became bored and distressed by the repetitiveness of the expected teaching style. Paul said "I don't feel like I'm teaching. I feel like a trained English monkey, getting up there, and I say, 'please repeat it.' That's not truly acquiring a language." He felt "a little guilty," because the company charged their clients an enormous sum of money. Michael criticised the company, which, despite its pretence of caring about the students, it actually treated them as "ATMs for the company." He described his previous employer as "McDonald's English School," where "they have the cheapest lessons they could give you, … in the quickest amount of time." As for the hiring criteria, "It's not about education skills. It's about what you can market."

Despite such frustration, Paul found it fascinating to find out that one male student, who had been silent for a long time, finally opened his mouth to reveal that he had visited 27 countries. Paul acknowledged that talking about such topics was difficult for low-level students, but he said, "I learned one thing – how much you can communicate with just a few words and phrases."

For both Michael and Paul, teaching eikaiwa seemed to be a temporary job. Michael was still exploring his career and mentioned about going back to school and "get a degree in English literature, maybe Ph.D." Conversely, Paul was already planning to go back to school for a nursing degree and license. As white, male, native speakers of English with higher education, these men were privileged. These teachers' employment tends to contribute to the structure of the eikaiwa world, filled with problematic ideologies and inequities. Nevertheless, the eikaiwa world cannot be fully understood without knowing their stories of despair, concern, and desire.

This ground-breaking book illuminates this other side of the eikaiwa world by uncovering the diverse yet hidden voices of eikaiwa teachers. Their stories of marginalities, ambitions, and possibilities help us understand how these teachers pursue their careers as professionals, engage in education, and negotiate challenges.

Acknowledgements

We have to start by expressing our deepest thanks to our series editors, Diane Hawley Nagatomo and Melodie Cook for expertly guiding us through this process and being a constant source of encouragement and support - we would have been lost without them! We also wish to show our appreciation to Jo Mynard from Candlin & Mynard ePublishing. Jo was a treasure trove of knowledge and advice as well as just being a fantastic person who puts so much effort into helping everyone around her. Without all of these people expressing their confidence in us, this project would certainly never have been possible or even conceived of.

We are also greatly indebted to our contributing authors. From the very beginning, we have been blown away by their professionalism and work ethic and are delighted with the fascinating insights into eikaiwa that they have given us access to. They have all made our lives so much easier as editors and we are extremely grateful! We have no doubt that their voices will have a profoundly positive impact on the lives of many eikaiwa teachers and students.

A special thanks must also go to Ryuko Kubota for believing in our project, kindly agreeing to contribute our foreword, and for her expert advice. Her work on eikaiwa was the catalyst for many of us to explore this industry more deeply and she continues to have a crucial role in making language education in Japan fairer and more inclusive.

Daniel: I want to thank my wonderful and supportive wife, Mayu. Without your help I wouldn't have been able to do any of this. Thanks to my little buddies, Hayato and Takuma, for cheering me up and motivating me to keep on writing when I might not want to! Also, to my mum, Joy, thank you for giving me the chances that you didn't have, I'll always appreciate it. Finally, to my dad, Peter - I love you and miss you every day.

Natasha: I would like to thank Dr. Christine Pearson Casanave and Dr. Eton Churchill for the help and encouragement I have received from them. Chris has been very generous with her time and provided me with invaluable advice during my research every step of the way. Dr. Eton Churchill believed in my research project from the start and helped me tremendously with the research design and initial revisions.

I would also like to thank my husband Katsushi and daughter Ines for being supportive and patient during all those long hours I spent researching and writing.

About the editors

DANIEL HOOPER has been living and teaching in Japan since 2005. He worked within the eikaiwa industry for eight years in a large chain school and in a small-family owned eikaiwa. He has worked as a full-time instructor in the English Language Institute at Kanda University of International Studies since April 2017. He received his MA TESOL from Kanda University of International Studies in 2016. His research interests are teacher and learner identity, native-speakerism, learner autonomy, and issues related to the eikaiwa industry.

NATASHA HASHIMOTO, currently a PhD candidate at Temple University, has lived in Japan for 17 years. She worked in eikaiwa and cram schools (*juku*) for several years. Currently, she teaches in the English Language Department at Tokyo Woman's Christian University. She received her master's degree in Human Rights (research track) from Arizona State University in 2010. Her research interests include language assessment, migration, and labour and human rights issues in ELT. She won two research grants for eikaiwa research in 2017/2018.

Contributing authors

BOON, ANDREW Andrew Boon is a professor in the faculty of Global Communications at Toyo Gakuen University, Tokyo. He started life in Japan as a GEOS eikaiwa teacher for four years. He now holds a PhD in Applied Linguistics, has presented at numerous conferences, and has published many articles in the field.

CATER, MARTIN Martin Cater has been living and teaching in Japan since 2004. During this time, he has been a Senior Teacher at a metropolitan branch of a large eikaiwa chain, a teacher at private and national universities, an examiner, and a private English tutor. He holds a Trinity LTCL DipTESOL certificate and an MA in Applied Linguistics from the University of Birmingham, UK. His research interests include native-speakerism, language teaching methodology, and learner autonomy.

IIDA, RUTH Ruth Iida moved to Japan's Kanagawa Prefecture in 1999 and opened a small eikaiwa school in Hadano City that same year. After 16 years of teaching, she closed the school in order to return to school herself at Tokyo's Temple University. After receiving her MS in Education in 2017, she re-opened her language school with a revamped curriculum and distinctly new teaching style. Her interests include storytelling, music in the EFL classroom, and curriculum development for young learners.

ITO, LESLEY Lesley Ito is a well-known teacher, teacher trainer, school owner, and award-winning ELT materials writer based in Nagoya, Japan. She has taught in Japan since 1992, and is the owner of BIG BOW English Lab, an eikaiwa school for children with a CLIL curriculum and a strong focus on literacy. She received her MSc in Teaching Young Learners from Aston University in 2018 and is the current publications chair of the School Owners SIG in JALT.

JONES, MARC Marc Jones has worked in Japan from 2003 to 2006 and since 2008. Of his total time in Japan, eight years included time employed in chain eikaiwa schools. He holds the Trinity Diploma in TESOL and MA TESOL & Applied Linguistics from the University of Portsmouth, UK. His interests are listening, pronunciation and phonology, corpus linguistics for ESP, task-based language teaching, and teachers' beliefs regarding classroom practices.

KIERNAN, PATRICK Patrick Kiernan taught in eikaiwa schools for ten years to learners of all ages and is currently Associate Professor at Meiji University in the School of Business Administration. He has a PhD in Applied Linguistics from the University of Birmingham. His current research interests include multimodal and narrative discourse analysis of identities in education, business and online media.

LAWRENCE, LUKE Luke has been teaching in Japan since 2002. During this time he has taught in a wide variety of contexts, including five years at a major eikaiwa chain as both an instructor and manager. He is currently teaching at Yokohama City University and his research interests include issues pertaining to teacher identity, native-speakerism, whole-class group dynamics, use of L1 in the classroom and a range of critical issues in ELT.

LOWE, ROBERT Robert J. Lowe began his career in the Japanese eikaiwa industry in 2008, and later moved into university teaching. He is currently a lecturer in the Department of English Communication at Tokyo Kasei University, where he teaches undergraduate language and linguistics courses, and leads seminars in the graduate school. He holds a diploma in TESOL, as well as an MA and a PhD in Applied Linguistics. His research interests include native-speakerism in ELT, and qualitative research methods in applied linguistics.

MACDONALD, EWEN Ewen MacDonald is a lecturer in the English Language Institute at Kanda University of International Studies where he also completed his MA TESOL degree. He previously taught at junior/senior high school, on an English program at a cram school, as well as teaching eikaiwa classes to adults. His research interests include pragmatics, teacher cognition, learner autonomy and corrective feedback.

MASCHIO, CHRISTOPHER Christopher Maschio worked in the Business English division of a large eikaiwa school chain in Tokyo from 2003 to 2019. He has experience as a full-time business English instructor, language assessor, and material development specialist. His professional interests are extensive listening and task-based language teaching. He is currently teaching in Tokyo at a private language school and is a part-time lecturer at Hosei University. He holds an MA TESOL from Kanda University of International Studies, Japan.

NUSKE, KYLE Kyle Nuske is a Designated Associate Professor at Nagoya University. After teaching at a major eikaiwa chain for two years, he enrolled in the Composition & TESOL program at Indiana University of Pennsylvania and completed his doctoral degree in 2014. His research interests include critical teacher education and ideologies of English in Japan.

YARWOOD, AMELIA Amelia Yarwood completed her MA Linguistics (TESOL) at Sophia University, Japan, during which she worked as an eikaiwa instructor and junior high school teacher. Having graduated in 2018, she now continues to work in Japan as a Learning Advisor at Kanda University of International Studies. She does research in the areas of L2 Motivation, learner autonomy, language learner strategies and classroom-based practice.

Glossary

ALT
Assistant Language Teacher - A common entry-level position for generally untrained foreign language teachers. ALTs may work in elementary, junior high, or high schools in Japan and are generally expected to assist the certified Japanese Teacher of English with lesson planning and instruction. There are two main types of ALTs: those that work in the government-sponsored JET program and those that are employed by independent dispatch companies.

CELTA
Certificate in English Language Teaching to Adults - a widely recognised initial teacher training qualification for EFL/ESL teachers

Charisma Man
A character from a satirical comic strip series based on stereotypes of overconfident Caucasian males in Japan (Rodney & Garscadden, 2002). Originally a 'loser' in his home country, when Charisma Man arrives in Japan, he transforms into an attractive 'superhero' seemingly desired as a romantic partner by all Japanese women. Western women are portrayed as Charisma Man's archenemy as they can see his true nature thus causing all of his 'powers' to disappear.

CLT
Communicative Language Teaching

EFL/ ESL
English as a Foreign/ Second Language

ELT
English Language Teaching

Inner circle countries
Derived from Kachru's (1985) model of three concentric 'circles' (inner, outer, and expanding) of World English, inner circle countries are those in which English is the mother tongue for most people. Some examples of inner circle countries are the United Kingdom, the United States, Canada, Australia, New Zealand, and Ireland.

JALT
The Japan Association for Language Teaching – A non-profit organisation for language teachers in Japan with approximately 3,000 members both in Japan and overseas. The mission of JALT is to promote "excellence in language learning, teaching, and research by providing opportunities for those involved in language education to meet, share, and collaborate" (JALT, n.d.).

L1/ L2
A person's 1st/ 2nd language

MA
Master of Arts

MEXT
(Japanese) Ministry of Education, Culture, Sports, Science, and Technology

native-speakerism
A prevalent ideology in ELT centred around the belief that 'native speaker' teachers from Western inner circle countries represent the ideal in terms of both a language model and exponents of 'superior' English language teaching methodology (Holliday, 2006).

NEST/ NNEST
Native English Speaking Teacher/ Non-Native English Speaking Teacher

PPP
Presentation, Practice, Production: A widely utilised ELT methodology/framework based on 1) teachers presenting a grammar/vocabulary point, 2) providing controlled practice activities based on that point, and 3) giving freer activities for learners to produce language (including the target point) in a meaningful way.

TESOL
Teaching English to Speakers of Other Languages

TOEIC
Test Of English for International Communication - an internationally recognised standardised test designed to measure English skills for use in an international environment. There are currently two varieties of test: 1) reading and listening and 2) speaking and writing.

SLA
Second Language Acquisition

Japanese terms

akogare

Often translated into English as 'desire', 'yearning' or 'longing', this term is often used in the academic literature on eikaiwa schools to describe the sexualised or aspirational desire of Japanese women for Caucasian Western men (Kubota, 2011a; Takahashi, 2013). More recently, however, Nonaka (2018) has defined the term in more general terms as "a sentiment in which we desire to pursue our dreams whether they be a person or an object (tangible or intangible) that is tantalizingly out of reach from us" (pp. 4-5).

eikaiwa gakkou

English conversation school

Eiken

The Eiken Test in Practical English Proficiency (実用英語技能検定 *Jitsuyō Eigo Ginō Kentei*) - a well-known major English test conducted throughout Japan and backed by MEXT. The test assesses all four skills (reading, writing, speaking, and listening) and is recognised by many schools and universities as part of their entrance requirements for English proficiency.

gaijin

Literally translated as "outside person" or "outsider," this is a Japanese word for foreigners or non-Japanese. There is some debate over whether the word is neutral or has a pejorative tone. There is also a more formal term - *gaikokujin* - which simply refers to a non-Japanese foreign national.

genki

Roughly translated as "energy", "vigour", or "pep." Among some English teachers in Japan, there is a belief that many ELT jobs prize a teacher's "*genki*ness" or liveliness over other factors such as teaching experience, qualifications, or general professionalism (Bailey, 2007; Gay, 2009).

juku

Cram schools found in almost every town and city in Japan that offer supplementary classes, predominantly for the purpose of helping students to pass secondary school and university entrance exams.

nihonjinron

An umbrella term for discourse on Japaneseness and the Japanese national character that commonly emphasises the idea that the Japanese language, culture, and race possess unique traits that stand in contrast to the values of the West (see, for example, Befu, 2001).

1. Moving beyond "McEnglish"

Daniel Hooper
Natasha Hashimoto

"I think that kind of stereotype or something about eikaiwa in some ways makes it difficult to say, to put your hand up with vigour, 'Yes, I did the eikaiwa thing.'"
(Eikaiwa teacher interviewed in Hooper, 2017)

Eikaiwa: What is it?

Although at times a tricky category to pin down, eikaiwa schools are, put simply, private businesses outside of formal education that provide English conversation classes and examination preparation for tests such as TOEFL or TOEIC. The Japanese commercial ELT sector is very large and is comprised of both smaller schools owned by one person (who might also be the only teacher working in that particular school) and large chain schools, such as Aeon, Nova, and Gaba. This sector also includes the cottage eikaiwa industry, which is private eikaiwa teaching conducted by foreigners at their homes or other places, such as coffee shops or students' homes, that are convenient for them and their students to meet at (Nagatomo, 2013).

As previously stated, a common denominator for all eikaiwa schools, both small and large chain schools, is their existence "outside formal educational institutions" (Kubota, 2011a, p. 248). This private eikaiwa sector is extremely important as Japan is "one of the largest commercial markets for English language instruction in the world" (Galloway, 2014, p. 8).

"McEnglish": Eikaiwa as stigmatised and forgotten

Unsurprisingly, the considerable scale of the private ELT market in Japan has meant that the quality of eikaiwa lessons can vary greatly. Some schools, in particular those run by large chain companies, have gradually acquired a reputation as purveyors of dubious quality classes - the educational equivalent of junk food (Currie-Robson, 2015; McNeill, 2004; Oakland, 2010).

According to Merriam-Webster (n.d.), a "McJob" is "a low-paying job that requires little skill and provides little opportunity for advancement." This term has existed since the 1980s (CNN, 2003) and since that time, several pejorative "Mc" derivatives have been coined categorising low quality newspapers as "McPapers" (Pritchard, 1987), martial arts schools as "McDojos" (Martial Reviews, n.d.), and housing as "McMansions" (McMansion Hell, n.d.). An article from the UK paper, The Guardian (Ford, 2004), discussed how English teaching in Europe had now attained the status of "McJob" due to worsening working conditions and negative stereotyping surrounding the industry. One teacher based in Greece summed up the stigma attached to the ELT profession and its "McTeachers":

> Graduates can take a four-week course then bum around Europe for a year, pretending to teach. They don't take the job very seriously so consequently no one takes them very seriously, and we all get tarred with the same brush. (Ford, 2004)

The term "McEnglish" relates specifically to eikaiwa and was probably coined in a Japan Times article (McNeill, 2004) at arguably the height of the eikaiwa boom before the high-profile bankruptcy of major eikaiwa chains such as Nova and Geos in the late 2000s. Citing gruelling schedules, high staff turnover, and low wages, the author claimed that eikaiwa schools were picture-perfect representations of "McDonaldization." McDonaldization was a concept termed and analysed by the sociologist George Ritzer (2000), where he described how the highly standardised and controlled management of various institutions in society had come to resemble the way fast food restaurants are run. Throughout McNeill's "McEnglish" article, he strongly criticised eikaiwa schools, comparing them to fast-food restaurants, turning out lessons that are "about as nutritious as a bag of salty fries." The fast food metaphor is unfortunately one that has stuck, with expat online message boards categorising eikaiwa teachers as "Eikaiwa Mcmonkeys (sic)" (iza_kaiser (Reddit), 2015) and books like *English to Go* (Currie-Robson, 2015) sermonising on the lack of professionalism and quality inherent in the "McEnglish" (McNeill, 2004; Oakland, 2010) of eikaiwa. This grand narrative of eikaiwa as fast food English has, to date, been largely unchallenged in Japan and, as can be seen in the quotation at the start of this chapter, may lead teachers who have previously worked in the industry to conceal their eikaiwa "McHistory."

This leads us to why we have also chosen to describe eikaiwa in this section's heading as "forgotten." Due to the vast scale of the industry and the notoriety of chain schools like Nova in the public eye due to issues such as unpaid wages and unfulfilled student contracts (Japan Today, 2007; Stubbings, 2007), we realise that to some, the idea of eikaiwa being "forgotten" seems confusing or simply false. To clarify, what we are arguing is that within ELT in Japan, the value of eikaiwa as a legitimate educational context has been largely ignored. As a result, its role as an important source of learning for teachers and students has been forgotten.

In its official categorisation also, the eikaiwa industry has also been separated from formal language education. Private English schools are recognised as businesses and as such are under the overall administration of the Ministry of Economy, Trade and Industry (METI), whereas mainstream schools fall under the Ministry of Education, Culture, Sports, Science and Technology (MEXT). This business/education categorisation has contributed to a pejorative and unsound distinction made between "real" schools and eikaiwa, with the latter believed by many to be purely profit-focused at the expense of educational quality and standards (Aspinall, 2012; Nuske, 2014; Seargeant, 2009; Sapunaru Tamas, & Tamas, 2012). Even though Assistant Language Teachers (ALTs) in public schools generally have similar qualifications and experience to eikaiwa instructors, Makino (2015) has argued that eikaiwa is "seen as crasser because it is private enterprise" (p. 3). In addition, while critique of questionable business and educational practices in eikaiwa does have some value in highlighting improper business practices and exploitation within the industry, examples of good being done in these schools never make headlines or enter the public consciousness. This may have had the side effect of reinforcing eikaiwa's role as the "whipping boy" of Japanese ELT – an enduring epithet among expat teachers because of its role as a handy lightning rod for ills that arguably permeate the entire field.

It can also be said that, while eikaiwa is firmly accepted by the public as a place to study English, its position within the professional ELT community in Japan seems marginal at best. Whereas research on language learning, teacher identity, and interactions between learners or between learners and teachers in formal, traditional educational institutions (such as research on university teacher identity by Nagatomo, (2012); numerous publications on EFL pedagogy) as well as in cram schools (Dierkes, 2010; Entrich, 2018) is extensive, such research continues to be rare in the eikaiwa industry. There has been only a handful of studies with a focus on eikaiwa learners (Bailey, 2007; Hashimoto, 2013a, 2013b; Hooper, 2019b; Kubota, 2011a) and even a smaller number of studies that investigated eikaiwa teachers' identity and work conditions in eikaiwa schools (Appleby, 2013, 2014a; Galloway, 2014; Hooper, 2019a; Nagatomo, 2013). Although the eikaiwa industry is omnipresent and vast, not enough is known about it (Duff & Uchida, 1997; Nagatomo, 2013, 2016). Additional nuanced, theoretically sound, empirical research on the multifaceted, rich context of the eikaiwa sector is needed.

In addition to a marked lack of academic studies on eikaiwa schools (Lowe, 2015; Nagatomo, 2016), there is a substantial gap in terms of the scale of the industry and the extremely limited presence of eikaiwa teachers in professional teaching organisations such as the Japan Association for Language Teaching (JALT). Despite the number of eikaiwa instructors (both foreign and Japanese) in Japan standing at 10,301 in 2017 (METI, 2019), at the 2018 JALT International Conference, only eight out of over 650 presentations discussed the conversation/language school context and at the 2018 PanSIG Conference, out of 215 presentations, only three addressed the eikaiwa context. Although JALT is certainly not deliberately discouraging eikaiwa teachers from presenting, emic insights from eikaiwa schools are still not being heard. English Teachers in Japan (ETJ), another professional teaching organisation that offers low-cost conferences more accessible to teachers outside of tertiary education, does hold annual conferences that provide eikaiwa teachers more opportunities to present on pedagogy or research. However, despite the valuable work that this organisation is doing to create a professional community for teachers working in non-formal contexts, to date there are still few avenues for eikaiwa teachers to publish and share written accounts of what is going on in their classrooms and their working lives. Furthermore, teachers working outside of tertiary education have traditionally been transient and often not willing or able to write about their experiences (Caesar & Bueno, 2003). Of course, it is naive to assume that all (or even most) eikaiwa teachers desire any professional development opportunities. For many of those in the industry, the job is just a means to travel, party, or find themselves before returning to a "real" job in their home countries. There is certainly no shortage of "backpacker teachers" in eikaiwa schools. However, this is precisely why we feel that sharing voices of teachers who do not fit this model is important. There *are* teachers in eikaiwa who regard themselves as language teaching professionals and have been struggling to belong or make their voices heard. They may often find themselves in limbo – marginalised within formal educational circles and isolated within a working community which constantly undermines their need for a professional identity. Through this book we hope to show them that they are not alone and that their experiences have meaning and worth.

Considering the issues discussed above, we hope that the voices of the authors that comprise this book will go some way to changing the way people both inside and outside of eikaiwa regard the position of its teachers in Japanese ELT. Through this book, we aim to illuminate what we feel is another forgotten element of eikaiwa; the diversity that exists within the industry. In their collection of essays on the experiences of "native" English teachers in Japan, Caesar and Bueno (2003) acknowledge the problems inherent in trying to represent the reality of "native-speaker" eikaiwa teachers in one all-encompassing trope:

> Berlitz, Nova, and ECC are the largest and most visible names of a myriad of English language schools (some having several branches in local areas, some having only one) throughout Japan. Hundreds and hundreds of native speakers of English-Americans, Canadians, Australians, English-teach at these schools. What single teaching experience would presume to represent the rest? (Caesar & Bueno, 2003, pp. 14-15)

Rather than focusing solely on those—teachers and owners—who have contributed to the pejorative image of the industry, we also wish to draw attention to the individuals who refuse to conform to this negative narrative. Although we will certainly be raising problematic issues that exist in eikaiwa, we feel that we also have an obligation to give voice to the many teachers who, despite institutional and sociocultural constraints as well as a stigmatised position in the field, are sincerely endeavouring to help language learners develop their confidence and proficiency.

Eikaiwa's position in Japanese ELT

The eikaiwa sector employs thousands of teachers, bringing in billions of yen in revenues annually. This figure includes revenues from the aforementioned large chain eikaiwa schools and smaller eikaiwa schools. According to the Yano Research Institute (2016), the revenues from commercial language schools were over 340 billion yen in 2015, which excludes revenues from sales of teaching materials published and/or sold by these schools. However, the Ministry of Economy, Trade and Industry (METI, 2017) disclosed that the sales, excluding teaching materials, in foreign language conversation schools in 2016 overall were around 650 billion yen. Although these two reported values are very different, they nevertheless indicate that eikaiwa is clearly a multi-billion yen industry.

Whether in order to prepare for tests, acquire practical, communicative English skills, or for other reasons, many English language learners study in eikaiwa schools, as the large number of schools throughout the country indicates. The Research and Statistics Department of the Ministry of Economy, Trade and Industry (2017) reported that there were over 3,800 commercial language schools in 2016 in Japan. Chain eikaiwa schools, such as Aeon, ECC, and Shane, can boast over 200 branches in different regions of Japan. Schools report having large numbers of students (e.g., in ECC over 400,000 students enrolled in its schools, as disclosed on ECC's website).

As previously stated, in its origin and core, the eikaiwa industry is an entity separate from formal education. Indeed, arguably one of the main reasons for the existence and scale of the eikaiwa industry stems from a perceived lack of communicative English instruction in formal secondary education due to the dominance of test-focused English or *eigo* (Aspinall, 2012; Hiramoto, 2013). From the end of World War II, dissatisfaction with the English proficiency of Japanese high school and university graduates steadily grew, culminating in a number of educational reforms and more foreigners being employed as teachers (Nagatomo, 2016). Even today, despite the Ministry of Education, Culture, Sports, Science, and Technology's (MEXT) recent curriculum reform efforts, there is a perception that English instruction in formal education is extremely unlikely to produce competent English users (Seargeant, 2008). Hiramoto (2013) argued that this belief has led to English conversation practice becoming the charge of institutions outside of MEXT's jurisdiction. Nagatomo (2016) also described how the eikaiwa world has been driven by this idea from the 1940s up to the present day and how the industry has developed from being predominantly a luxury for well-healed urban dwellers to something more widely accessible for all. A dichotomy between the *eigo* dominant in Japanese schools as "Japanese English" and *eikaiwa* as "foreign English" (McVeigh, 2004) has also been claimed to be buttressed by discourses portraying "authentic" English as being solely the realm of "native speaker" teachers (Lowe & Pinner, 2016; Seargeant, 2009), often a key selling point for eikaiwa schools.

Eikaiwa has become an industry spreading not only in the corporate but also, more recently, the academic sector, through outsourced English language courses and dispatched teachers (Breaden, 2016). Recently, increasing numbers of dispatched eikaiwa teachers, typically bachelor's degree holders, teach English in regular schools, such as elementary and high schools and in higher education. Some of these teachers are in charge of for-credit courses in not only undergraduate but also graduate schools in Japan (Fukunaga, Hashimoto, Lowe, Unser-schutz, & Kusaka, 2018).

Although in this book we strongly argue for the educational legitimacy of English conversation schools, there are undeniably certain elements of eikaiwa classes that may be quite removed from language learning. Kubota's (2011) study has been arguably the most influential work examining eikaiwa as a leisure activity. In her investigation of eikaiwa students and owners, she found that rather than being based on "investment" (getting some kind of socioeconomic return for learners' efforts), students participating in eikaiwa classes appeared to be doing so as "consumption" (receiving pleasure from language learning as a leisure activity). A number of other studies have highlighted similar findings, showing that for some, successful language acquisition may even be a relatively insignificant issue compared to other motivations for attending eikaiwa schools such as for a hobby or for socialising with like-minded others (Brown, 2005; Duff & Uchida, 1997; Hooper, 2019b; Watson & MacDonald, 2010). Historically, it has also been claimed that eikaiwa provided an idealised, exotic vision of the West – an escapist fantasy that people could step into as respite from the demoralising hardships of post-war Japan (Nagatomo, 2016). Linked to this, an additional influence claimed to particularly drive female eikaiwa enrolment is *akogare*. *Akogare* is a Japanese term roughly translated as "desire" or "longing" for the unattainable (Kelsky, 2001; Nonaka, 2018), but within the academic literature on eikaiwa has been largely used to refer to Japanese women's desire for freedom and empowerment (Bailey, 2007; Kelsky, 2001; Kubota, 2011a; Takahashi, 2013). More specifically, *akogare* within eikaiwa often refers to a desire for future professional or social liberation from a Japanese patriarchy offered by an idealised "West" (characterised by eikaiwa schools filled with foreign faces) or a more eroticised longing for romantic encounters with foreign (and predominantly Caucasian) males. Eikaiwa schools have, therefore, been described as "host clubs" (Kubota, 2011a), "theme park(s)" (Hooper, Oka, & Yamazawa, 2020), and "wonderland(s)" (Bailey, 2006). A recent study by Tajima (2018) has also revealed an interesting example of "reverse" *akogare* among Japanese males studying in online eikaiwa schools with female Filipino teachers. Tajima found that participants viewed their female instructors in "intimate and romanticised" ways (p. 1) and tended to select teachers on the basis of them being "cute" as it would motivate them to go through the "bother" of learning English (p. 11). Rather than using such beliefs as a reason to disregard eikaiwa as a legitimate educational context, we see these complex and often problematic elements of eikaiwa as representative in many ways of Japanese ELT as a whole (Hooper, 2018) and a powerful justification to explore the industry more thoroughly.

Eikaiwa: The Good, the Bad, and the Ugly

Legitimate roles for eikaiwa

Despite the "McJob" label that many have assigned to the eikaiwa industry, eikaiwa schools can and do represent legitimate sites for language learning. The significant demand for eikaiwa classes highlighted earlier in this chapter can be explained in part by eikaiwa schools' position as one of the only available destinations for Japanese post-tertiary English learners. Perhaps due to Japan being an EFL context, few opportunities exist for everyday engagement with English and, owing to the absence of a community college system in Japan, eikaiwa is one of the few adult education options available for those wishing to continue English studies after university (Makino, 2016; McVeigh, 2002). A handful of small-scale studies have illustrated cases where eikaiwa has operated as a site for effective learner development. In one case study based on the diary entries of an eikaiwa learner (Hooper, 2019b), the student displayed a remarkable level of commitment to language learning tied to a desire to move closer to her ideal L2 self (Dörnyei, 2009) – a member of an imagined community of international English users (Norton, 2001). In a study of four learners in an eikaiwa school, Hashimoto (2013b) also presented a more complex picture of the eikaiwa classroom as a site with potential for both meaningful language learning and personal growth. Although with a slightly different focus, another study (Hashimoto 2013a) presented another aspect of an evolving eikaiwa school where Japanese ELLs interacted with other non-native English speakers (learners of Japanese as a second language) using English as a Lingua Franca to communicate in multicultural exchange sessions.

Focusing on the potentially positive influence of eikaiwa on teachers, a recent study (Hooper, 2019b) found that the wide variety of eikaiwa student demographics and motivations was perceived by former eikaiwa teachers to have had a substantial influence on their professional development. Many participants, all of whom had transitioned from eikaiwa into university teaching, stated that their experiences in eikaiwa classrooms fostered flexibility and reactivity to learner needs. Additionally, several of the teachers in this study stated that their experiences in eikaiwa had shaped their teacher identity, leading them to realise the considerable value of more egalitarian interpersonal relationships in the classroom. Some teachers also felt that university English education could actually benefit from adopting some of the practices commonplace in eikaiwa including a greater focus on one-on-one student counselling.

Benefits for teachers

There are a number of benefits to eikaiwa employment that have been reported in earlier research and discussed in online forums. Some teachers might come to Japan in order to work in eikaiwa schools because it is an adventure for them (Currie-Robson, 2014a). Some eikaiwa schools capitalise on this, advertising ELT jobs as a chance for foreign teachers to see the world and enjoy other cultures. For example, Gaba, a large chain eikaiwa school, recruits potential teachers with phrases such as "no experience required" and offers them "[a] rich history and unique culture mix with the ultra modern in the cities of Japan," adding that "there's something here to enjoy for everyone" (Gaba, n.d.).

Teaching private eikaiwa classes can also offer a great deal of scheduling flexibility. Nagatomo (2013) found this to be the most widely cited advantage of eikaiwa teaching in her study of homemaker teachers working in the cottage eikaiwa industry as respondents stated that they needed to be able to balance their work and family responsibilities. Flexibility also extended to not being directly employed by any company, meaning they had the freedom to choose the style of teaching that they believed was most effective and also the power to turn away any difficult students if necessary.

An important issue for any job is remuneration. From the information that is available on pay in the eikaiwa sector, it would not be a surprise to hear that many young eikaiwa teachers are relatively satisfied with their salaries. That is because eikaiwa jobs tend to pay more than many other part-time or contract jobs in Japan. From searching through *gaijinpot.com* (a job search website mainly for foreign nationals in Japan), one can find that many, if not most eikaiwa schools currently advertise ELT jobs paying between 2,000 and 3,000 yen per hour, with some offering significantly more. Teachers who had arrived in Japan in the early 1990s, saw eikaiwa work as well-paid and "one of the easiest jobs" (Appleby, 2014a, p. 42). As numerous online posts indicate (e.g., the comments below an online article by Mascetti, in *Japan Today*, 2018), some teachers worry that low income or unemployment in their home countries would lead to less fulfilling life styles, so they might be more content doing eikaiwa jobs in Japan.

The dark side of eikaiwa

The little existing literature suggests that eikaiwa work is stigmatised and the industry discriminatory. Some of Appleby's (2013) research participants reported feeling devalued and dissatisfied with their unstable jobs, which Taylor's (2017) research confirms. In addition to confirming problems with unstable jobs and poor working conditions, Hashimoto (2014a) found that many Japanese and foreign NNESTs (nonnative English-speaking teachers) felt discriminated against. Their L1, national background, and/or race tended to be negatively perceived by certain employers. In a similarly problematic situation were NESTs of Asian descent. These teachers, despite coming from English-speaking countries, also found that they experienced racial discrimination in the Japanese eikaiwa industry (Hashimoto, 2014b). In addition to these issues, Hooper and Snyder (2017) discuss the de-professionalisation of teachers in eikaiwa. Indicative of how the industry is negatively perceived in broader contexts are words a participant in Hooper's (2017) study used to describe his eikaiwa work experience: "a black cloud [over my career]." It may not be surprising then that Nagatomo (2016) has qualified eikaiwa jobs as the least prestigious type of ELT work in Japan. Despite the more positive approach to eikaiwa that we adopt in this book, we believe it is crucial that the discrimination and abuse that continues in the industry is also foregrounded and discussed honestly.

Of course, eikaiwa's bad reputation did not materialise from thin air – many schools and teachers have rightly earned the stigma and notoriety applied to the industry. There has been much discussion about the negative aspects of eikaiwa concerning discrimination and legal abuses. A reader of the Japan Today online newspaper posted a message saying that eikaiwa schools were "glorified sweatshops" (*Japan Today*, 2015). It has also been reported that eikaiwa schools do not enrol their employees in legally mandatory social insurance schemes (*Zooming Japan*, 2013). Over the years, newspaper articles, particularly in *The Japan Times*, have also featured stories about decreasing standards of working conditions in the commercial ELT industry, including instances of illegal dismissal, increasingly inflexible work schedules, decrease in payment, unpaid work, and sexual harassment (for example, Currie-Robson, 2014a, 2014b, 2016; Kikuchi, 2017; McCrostie, 2014; St. Michel, 2015). Many of these incidents have been reported on the General Union website as well (General Union, n.d.). In addition, memoirs written by current and former eikaiwa teachers (for example, Brotherstone, 2014; Currie-Robson, 2015) include stories about problems in the eikaiwa industry that have also been discussed in the popular press and online forums. In Currie-Robson's "*English To Go*" (2015), some of the more shocking recounts of the "heyday" of eikaiwa included one young instructor calling a student "a wanker" after the student complained that he was not given a chance to speak in class, and another male teacher engaging in sex with a high school-age student during home lessons.

Narratives

We have chosen to adopt a narrative approach as the primary research method in this volume for various reasons. Firstly, narrative research has already proven to be effective in investigating teachers' professional lives (Clandinin & Connelly, 2000; Nagatomo, 2012; 2016; Tsui, 2007; Duff & Uchida, 1997) because of its usefulness for "understand[ing] phenomena from the perspective of those who experience them" (Barkhuizen, Benson, & Chik, 2014, p. 2). Drawing from this, there has been a call for greater narrative-focused research in the area of language teacher identity (Barkhuizen, 2017).

Furthermore, as this volume is specifically focusing on English education in eikaiwa, we feel it is important that we take a qualitative/narrative perspective because it allows for a focus on the particularities of a certain context (Barkhuizen, 2013; Clandinin & Connelly, 2000). The importance of context in narrative studies is emphasised by Reissman (2008) who stated, "Stories don't fall from the sky… they are composed and received in contexts – interactional, historical, institutional, and discursive – to name a few" (p. 105). We feel that context cannot be separated from either language teaching or learning and that a narrative approach will allow us to give the idiosyncrasies of eikaiwa the attention they require.

An important caveat when discussing narratives is researcher positionality, i.e. "their world view and their chosen position in relation to a specific research task" (Heath, 2018, p. 73). We believe that the position of our contributors as current or former "insider" perspectives (Heath, 2018) is a strength of this volume as it provides emic perspectives that have been largely absent on the topic of eikaiwa. However, these stories represent subjective interpretations of events, shaped by each author's unique biases and values. In this sense, each chapter is not dealing with objective or generalisable "facts." Instead, it is 'points of connection' (Barkhuizen et al., 2014) – stories that the reader can relate to and connect with their own unique situation – that we aim to provide in this volume.

Finally, we believe that by focusing on teachers' stories told in their own words, we will be able to maintain readability and be engaging for not only researchers, but also practicing teachers in eikaiwa looking to gain a deeper understanding of their teaching context. Narrative studies "expand the range of voices that are heard in research reports, often highlighting the experiences of marginalised groups outside of the academy" (Barkhuizen et al., 2014, p. 3). Due to the aforementioned lack of academic attention towards eikaiwa and a continued stigmatisation of the eikaiwa industry both in TESOL and in Japanese society (Appleby, 2013; Lummis, 1976; McNeill, 2004), we believe that a narrative approach is necessary to draw attention to the lived experiences of teachers. By foregrounding eikaiwa teachers' voices, we hope to challenge prevalent unconstructive stereotypes and raise awareness of important social issues within this educational sector.

Outline of this book

In this book there are three sections that address the various issues surrounding eikaiwa that were raised in this introduction. The first section of the book focuses on critical issues in eikaiwa. More specifically, four authors take on critical perspectives relating to the nature of eikaiwa teaching and its often problematic and essentialised portrayal in academia and society. Drawing on their lived experiences as teachers and researchers, the authors unpack a number of critical issues such as native-speakerism, racism, and nationalism that surreptitiously infiltrate many daily practices in eikaiwa (and more generally Japanese ELT).

Getting critical

In chapter 2, Robert Lowe draws on his concept of the "native speaker frame" to analyse three mini-stories from his time as an eikaiwa teacher in order to foreground the implicit native-speakerism that permeates institutional policy and teachers' attitudes in some eikaiwa schools. His stories and the concerning implications that they suggest reinforces a need for awareness raising of "common-sense" prejudice in both eikaiwa and the TESOL field globally.

Through a narrative telling of his journey as an eikaiwa teacher and researcher, Daniel Hooper takes on the issue of "fun" or "leisure" within eikaiwa teaching in chapter 3. He claims that while the notion of eikaiwa teachers being "fun" is often marked as cause for eikaiwa being positioned outside of "serious" education, the socially-constructed identity of the "entertainer" is by no means restricted to eikaiwa. Furthermore, he also argues that "fun" has undeservedly been given a bad name in the field and that, even in the face of social/professional stigma, eikaiwa teachers can craft their own valid "educator" identities.

In chapter 4, through examining the narratives of over forty teachers, Natasha Hashimoto delves into the complex issues facing migrant (non-Japanese) NNESTs, including herself, working in the eikaiwa industry. This chapter goes into detail on the complex working situations that many migrant NNESTs experience and the various ways in which they negotiate discrimination and instability within eikaiwa schools.

In chapter 5, focusing on his experiences and research on the apparent interaction between native-speakerism and nationalism, Martin Cater addresses how learner beliefs in eikaiwa can be shaped by larger influences from the ELT industry and Japanese society. He discusses how native-speakerism and the Japanese nationalist ideology of *nihonjinron* can be seen in the stated beliefs of Japanese English learners and how these ideas are sometimes promoted by eikaiwa schools. However, he also gives examples from his personal experience of how these problematic ideologies can be disrupted through grassroots action by teachers.

Negotiating pedagogy

The second section of this book features five chapters in which the authors explore the multifaceted nature of eikaiwa pedagogy and the rarely-reported idiosyncrasies and challenges that eikaiwa teachers negotiate in the classroom. In these stories, we are confronted with the complexity that eikaiwa teachers face in balancing their principles against the contextual demands of the industry. We also learn about the ways in which eikaiwa teachers work to craft legitimate professional identities for themselves.

In chapter 6, Lesley Ito provides insight into the tensions that she must negotiate as an eikaiwa owner in responding to demands from parents that clash with her teacher beliefs. She describes how she has been able to use her professional expertise to negotiate these difficulties. She also shows why, due to her concern for the wellbeing of young learners at her school, she has continued to resist "common-sense" assumptions on standardised testing from parents and society-at-large.

Amelia Yarwood deals with the issue of emotional labour in chapter 7 where she relates stories from four teachers (including herself) that focus on the deeply complex and emotionally taxing work that eikaiwa teachers are sometimes called upon to do. These narratives reveal a wide-ranging collection of identities that eikaiwa teachers are asked to inhabit including coach, psychologist, and service provider, and the emotional toll that these often-contradictory roles take on teachers.

In chapter 8, Chris Maschio draws on over ten years of experience in both business English and eikaiwa and challenges a number of prevalent assumptions about these teaching contexts. He paints a detailed and nuanced picture of the realities of teaching as an eikaiwa or business English instructor while also noting how these educational sectors have evolved over the last two decades.

In chapter 9, Ruth Iida describes her journey as an eikaiwa owner establishing her own school and subsequently going through her MA TESOL studies. Her story reveals the gradual evolution of a teacher's beliefs as well as highlighting her earnest desire to help her students develop. She describes how she was able to bring her teaching practice more in line with findings from TESOL research while ensuring buy in from the community of learners/clients that financially supported her school.

In chapter 10, Ewen MacDonald compares eikaiwa and *juku* (cram schools), arguably the two most overlooked contexts in TESOL research in Japan. Having simultaneously worked in both contexts, he relates the affordances and constraints he experienced in each classroom and explores the ways in which he feels his experiences in eikaiwa and *juku* contributed to his evolving teacher identity.

Professional identity and growth

In the third section of the book we introduce five chapters in which the authors focus on the diverse and numerous ways that eikaiwa teaching has impacted teachers' identity construction and professional development. Through these deeply personal perspectives on their lived experiences, the authors illustrate the critical and enduring role that their time in eikaiwa has had in shaping their teaching careers. These deeply analytical narrative perspectives problematise the simplistic "McJob" tag that has been ascribed to eikaiwa and show that many teachers have the will and the means to grow as professionals within these contexts.

Marc Jones discusses his story of professional growth in a large chain eikaiwa school in chapter 11 and the affordances for training, reflection, and observation that he was able to capitalise on during the early stages of his career. Through his personal experiences in eikaiwa, Marc presents provides examples of ways in which he was able to proactively utilise the resources around him to stimulate his own pedagogical growth in a teaching environment lacking in formalised professional development opportunities.

In chapter 12, Luke Lawrence takes the reader through his experiences of training in eikaiwa and problematises prevalent perceptions of eikaiwa teachers being ineffective due to the fact that they commonly lack standardised teaching qualifications. He also describes the substantial role that he perceives eikaiwa to have had in his development as an educator over a ten-year career in Japan. In this chapter, he scrutinises a number of widely-held assumptions about the superior utility and relevance of Western-centric qualifications such as CELTA and TESOL as opposed to in-house training grounded in the local realities of the eikaiwa classroom.

Through two distinct perspectives on careers in eikaiwa, in chapter 13 Patrick Kiernan presents two very different but equally complex narratives illustrating the professional identity development of long-term eikaiwa teachers. The lived experiences of these two professionals reveals a great deal about the ways in which teachers negotiate multiple desired and undesired identities over the course of their careers. The complexity found in these teacher narratives provides a convincing counter perspective to the overly simplistic and often derogatory way that the professional lives of eikaiwa teachers are framed in both the ELT field and Japanese society at large.

In chapter 14, Kyle Nuske's narrative documents his gradual evolution as a critically-aware educator throughout his journey as a young, inexperienced eikaiwa teacher up to his present position as a university professor. He shows how he became increasingly aware of a number of questionable critical issues and assumptions in his particular eikaiwa teaching context and that his heightened consciousness of race, gender, and sexuality in ELT had a huge impact on developing professional identity. Additionally, he found that the pedagogical skill set cultivated during his time in eikaiwa aided him in introducing analysis of the same critical issues to his university students in a nuanced and respectful way.

In chapter 15, the final chapter of this section, Andy Boon examines the future careers of those who worked in and departed from the eikaiwa industry. He draws upon both his own experience and the stories of ten former eikaiwa teachers who are currently working in fields as diverse as banking, public relations, and photography. The stories in this chapter highlight a number of transferable skills that experience in eikaiwa provided these individuals and how they were able to utilise them in their different professional sectors. His insights challenge the predominantly negative framing of eikaiwa by focusing on the growth that can occur through working in the industry.

Chapter 16, "What can we learn from eikaiwa?", is the final chapter of this volume. Here, we summarise and unpack the main themes that emerged from the fourteen chapters and what implications they have for the future of eikaiwa and its position within our field. By reflecting on the stories shared throughout this book, we challenge prevalent stereotypes associated with eikaiwa, emphasise the complexity of eikaiwa teachers' lived experiences, and discuss unresolved issues in the industry that need to be addressed in future eikaiwa research.

Part 1: Getting critical

2. Exploring "native speaker" framing in eikaiwa

Robert J. Lowe

This chapter focuses on the operation of *the 'native speaker' frame* in Japanese eikaiwa schools. The construct of the 'native speaker' frame builds on Holliday's (2005, 2006) concept of native-speakerism, which refers to the ways in which Western institutions and those practitioners perceived to be "native speakers"[1] are privileged in global English language teaching (ELT). Borrowing from Feagin's (2013) work on white racial framing in the study of systemic racism, the 'native speaker' frame is intended to expand on Holliday's concept, focusing on the ways in which ELT theory and practice is interpreted through a Western "native speaker" lens, subtly allowing "native"-normativity to become accepted within the field. "Native-normativity" here refers to the idea that teachers and speakers of English should adhere to linguistic and pedagogical standards defined by the "native speaker" West. This leads to a commonly-adopted "native speaker"-centric outlook, which "assumes the superiority and normativity of Western educational technology and views the rest of the world from a viewpoint of educational and cultural deficiency" (Lowe, forthcoming). The "native speaker" frame is constructed and supported by common professional discourses in ELT, which serve to uphold notions that, through reinforcement, become hegemonic (i.e. considered to be common-sense by the majority of practitioners). As Holliday (2018) has noted, discourses are specific and powerful ways of speaking within groups, which "draw people into the thinking which underpins them" (p. 118). In terms of native-speaker framing, these discourses include (but are not limited to) the following:

- **The idealised image of the Western "native speaker"** – the idea that the Western "native speaker" is the ideal speaker, model, and teacher of English.

---

[1] I choose here to place the term "native speaker" in quotation marks to indicate that within ELT it is a largely socially constructed category applied to speakers on the basis of non-linguistic factors such as race and nationality (Davies, 2003), and is therefore to be understood as ideological and socially-constructed, rather than as a piece of objective terminology (see Holliday, 2005).

- **Western methodological normativity** – the belief that communicative ELT approaches developed in the "native speaker" West are by definition superior to the teaching methods used in non-Western educational settings, which are deviant from this norm.
- **Non-Western methodological and educational inferiority** – the notion that non-Western approaches to ELT are by definition inferior to Western communicative approaches, a belief which is often justified through simplistic and stereotypical portrayals of the teaching and learning going on in non-Western classrooms.
- **Cultural deficiency among students** – the cultural stereotyping of students using negative (or negatively-inflected) adjectives such as "collectivist," "passive" and "uncritical." Belief in this idea of "cultural deficiency" causes to teachers to promote things such as "active learning," "critical thinking," and so on. The promotion of such ideas risks being patronising and offensive to students, because it assumes that non-Western students are incapable of these things without the intervention of foreign ELT experts.

In addition to these large and common discourses, there are other more context-specific discourses which serve the same ends – that is, bolstering Western "native speaker" normativity, and positioning non-Western colleagues and students as problematic Others who are in need of correction, or whose views can be safely ignored. In other words, the "native speaker" frame can be thought of as "a perceptual filter used to view the ELT industry through the lens of the Western "native speaker" and the educational technology and values such a speaker is thought to embody" (Lowe, forthcoming). This framing is created and reinforced through common discourses in ELT, such as those outlined above, and it is therefore through a critical examination of such discourses that this framing can be identified and challenged.

Exploring "native speaker" framing in eikaiwa

It is no secret that eikaiwa schools are generally very "native speaker"-centric, with "native speaker" teachers often a selling point of a school or a chain (Seargeant, 2009). However, there has been little work on the more implicit discourses that exist within eikaiwa schools, serving to propagate and uphold "native speaker" framing. Recent work on native-speakerism has included autobiographical elements in order to explore problematic discourses and the experiences of teachers (see Gagné, Herath, & Valencia, 2018; Lowe & Kiczkowiak, 2016; Lowe & Lawrence, 2018; Warren & Park, 2018), and considering the prevalence of eikaiwa in Japan, it seems there is an opportunity for such approaches to provide rich and detailed insights into the operation of this ideology in the private sector.

In this chapter, I will draw on my own experiences of teaching in eikaiwa in order to draw attention to some of these discourses. I will then seek to reinterpret these experiences through a critical lens (i.e. by considering the ways that potentially stereotypical or native-speakerist assumptions influenced the choices and behaviours of the participants in each situation) (Denzin, 2013). The goal of doing so is to provide an exploration of the meanings of these events when considered in the context of the "native speaker" frame. This chapter will not provide a full account of my time working in eikaiwa, rather, it will provide short narrative vignettes, each highlighting an example of one or more of the discourses which I believe provide evidence of "native speaker" framing within the eikaiwa industry. These are of course only personal reflections, taken from several years in the past, and cannot be seen as wider evidence of "native speaker" framing in the industry. I hope, however, that through the examination of one teacher's experiences, others may be able to reinterpret their own encounters with such discourses through the same lens, and perhaps begin to critically question some of these discourses and the beliefs they signify.

Vignette 1:

When I first came to Japan I started working in a medium-sized eikaiwa chain. Teachers were assigned to a different school each day, and these could be located quite far apart. The schools in the city tended to be seen as the more prestigious postings, with a clientele of businessmen and the more well-to-do residents of the surrounding area. Teachers working in the branches in the suburbs were generally tasked with teaching groups of children or housewives.

As a new teacher, I primarily found myself working in the suburban schools, and my classes usually consisted of middle-aged housewives, who came to study either individually or in groups. The received wisdom about these students was that language learning was simply a hobby for them; something to get them out of the house while their husbands were at work. I often heard it said that these students were not planning to travel, nor to use the language in any meaningful way, and therefore these classes did not need to be taken all that seriously.

This is the way these classes were presented to me by colleagues and school managers, and this is the way I conducted them. I would often do very little preparation in advance of my lessons and would usually teach from the textbook almost verbatim, with snatches of conversation sprinkled in here and there when appropriate. I very rarely asked the students about their motivations for studying – after all, I already knew.

One day, as one of my group classes was leaving the room, one of the students paused in the doorway and said, in faltering English, "I go to abroad next month, is my English OK?" I had no idea how to answer the question. I had assumed her needs based on what I had been told about these students and had paid little attention to whether her language had developed in any significant way over the months she had been taking my class. "Yes, it's fine!" I cheerfully replied.

What does this mean?

It is not clear why this incident has stuck in my mind. On the surface, it is not particularly significant, nor did it lead to any sudden revelation about my teaching. After this event, I went on conducting my classes much as I had before. However, looking back at it now through a more critical lens, it seems clear that my beliefs and behaviour were influenced by some of the discourses described earlier. In particular, there seem to be assumptions here about cultural deficiency on the part of the students, and an arrogance on the part of the teacher. I had been told, and had believed, that these students were "just housewives" who learned languages as a hobby, and who were not actually interested in language learning for any "real" purpose (see Kubota, 2011a for a case-specific example of these discourses in the research literature). As such, I never took the time to find out the needs, the goals, or the desires of my students. I simply went ahead teaching in the way that I thought was best for them. Even worse, when a student did express her desires and her concerns about whether her language level was suitable for her needs, I lied and told her that her level was fine. At the time, I considered this both a positive thing and an act of self-preservation; her confidence would be boosted, and I would not have to face difficult questions about whether I was doing a good job as a teacher. However, under the surface it seems clear that I was reducing this student to a simplified Other, who was "just a housewife." I assumed I knew what her learning objectives were and did not consider them important. Even as I was presented with disconfirming evidence, I continued not to take the student seriously by deceiving her about her language level. This assumption throughout—that the students did not know what was good for them, and that I was able to make that decision for them—seems a clear example of a discourse of cultural inferiority influenced by "native speaker" framing.

Vignette 2:

In our company, students who were considering signing up for one of our courses were given a taiken *(demonstration) lesson. These lessons were about twenty minutes long, and were conducted using specially prepared materials, graded to different language levels. At the beginning of the taiken lesson, the teacher engaged in conversation with the student for about five minutes, in order to roughly gauge their language level. Following this, the teacher selected the worksheet which they felt was most appropriate for the student and led them through the activities. If a student successfully signed up to the school, the teacher would be given a bonus of 500 yen ("enough for a beer," as one trainer remarked).*

In my first year of teaching in eikaiwa, I was presented with a taiken student who had a very low level of English, and who kept attempting to speak to me in Japanese. I found this very irritating, as I did not know Japanese – this was an English school, after all! Still, I felt the lesson had gone quite well, and was hoping that the student would sign up for a course. Following the lesson, I learned from the school receptionist that the student had decided not to sign up. I was curious as to why not, and the receptionist explained that the student wanted a teacher who could speak Japanese, and who would be able to use some translation in their teaching.

I felt that this was ridiculous, and during my break spoke to some other teachers about what had happened. They agreed with my assessment, and when I mentioned that the student wanted a teacher who would speak Japanese, the idea was greeted with derisive snorts of "good luck!" We were also dismissive of the notion that a teacher might use translation in their lessons. Everyone knew that translation was wrong. It was one of the things we had learned on our training courses. The company itself discouraged the use of Japanese and made "English-only" a selling point in its advertising. The general mood was that we had dodged a bullet with this student.

What does this mean?

When first considering this incident, what struck me was the focus on methodological normativity, and the denigration of non-Western approaches to language teaching. Certainly, this is a theme here. The fact that my co-workers and I felt comfortable in dismissing the very idea of engaging in translation because we just knew it to be the "wrong" way to learn languages speaks to the strength of the discourse surrounding methodological approaches to ELT. This discourse, which considers Western communicative approaches to be superior to local methods by definition, made us feel confident that as representatives of the "native speaker" West we had the correct approach to language teaching, and that therefore any requests that relied on "unenlightened" methods such as translation could be safely discarded. This is not to say that communicative approaches are not effective in language instruction. Indeed, it is not even to claim that they are not *more* effective than other approaches. However, it is the chauvinistic dismissal of the requests of this student, from a group of teachers with very little training or experience, which strikes me as evidence of "native speaker" framing. We had not concluded that translation was bad based on a careful evaluation of evidence. We had done so on the basis of a received wisdom within the field; a discourse which allowed us to make strong judgements on which teaching methods were appropriate, and which were not, without the burden of actually having to check.

A second discourse which is evident in this vignette is the idea that we considered a student request for a Japanese-speaking teacher to be laughable. Once again, this speaks to the "English-only" assumptions of the field, and it also highlights an underexplored aspect of "native speaker" privilege. Speaking the language of the country in which a person is working is a minimal requirement for most jobs, and not doing so in many cases relegates even highly trained migrants to insecure, unskilled positions. The "English-only" discourse, in contrast, allows teachers to turn this weakness into a strength; their inability to speak the local language is interpreted as *making them a better teacher*, in much the same way as universities in Japan have preferred to hire foreign teachers as "pure and unacclimated aliens" whose lack of linguistic and cultural knowledge will allow students to get a "true" foreign cultural experience (Hall, 1998, p. 105). Indeed, as Phillipson (1992) has noted, monolingualism is one of the central fallacious assumptions that lies of the heart of much ELT practice. This attitude also results in Japanese eikaiwa teachers being disallowed from using their mother tongue, despite the recognised communicative and pedagogical benefits of judicious mother tongue use. I certainly do not wish to imply that such an attitude is shared by all English language teachers, nor all those from the Anglophone West. However, it was, as this vignette shows, a powerful discourse during my time working in eikaiwa, and one which reinforces "native speaker" normativity and privilege.

Vignette 3:

In one branch of the school, I had a class with six students, all of whom were women somewhere between early and late middle age. Some were housewives, some were working in office jobs, and two were language teachers, one in a junior high school, and one who worked on a volunteer basis at the local council. A class of six adults was unusually large for this school, and I saw it as an opportunity to employ some of the groupwork-style teaching I had learned and experienced during my CELTA training. I felt that the activities were quite successful, with the students happily discussing topics in pairs and groups and using the grammar they had been learning that day.

After the lesson, however, I faced a somewhat different reaction. The first comment came from another teacher in the branch, who had been watching part of the class through the glass panel in the door. "You don't want them learning from each other," she said, "they'll just pick up bad habits. If they're talking, they should be talking to you." The school owner was similarly critical, remarking that the students paid to come and talk to me, not to each other. I attempted to explain the reasoning behind my choice as a teacher, but the consensus seemed unbreakable; the students should be learning English from me, the "native speaker." If I continued using group and pair work, the students would learn "bad" English from each other, rather than "good" English from me. The following lesson I reluctantly returned to a teacher-fronted approach, in which all discussion centred on, and was filtered through me.

What does this mean?

This is a rather complex situation. What is immediately apparent is the focus on idealised "native speaker" norms of English. The comment from my co-worker—that the students would pick up "bad habits"—clearly reflects the idea that English use which was not heavily monitored and corrected by the teacher so as to conform to some kind of 'native' standard (though my own dialect of English is not exactly received pronunciation!) was inherently bad. As such, the class should be centred around me as a teacher; all spoken discourse passing through me as a form of "quality assurance." It seems very clear here that the school owner and my co-worker were engaging in a discourse which elevates the idealised "native speaker" to a very high position, and their English seen as the only acceptable outcome of language learning.

However, it is also possible to see some subversion here. I had attempted to use techniques such as pair work and group work which had been promoted on the CELTA course, and which have been identified by Holliday (2015) as "cultural icons" of ELT; i.e. activities which are engaged in almost ritualistically as part of the professional landscape of the field. The Japanese school owner could be read here as resisting the imposition of these activities in her school, instead making sure I taught in a way which was contextually appropriate. This may be seen as an example of resistance to "native speaker" framing, as the Western CLT approach I took was blocked and subverted by the school owner in favour of a more contextually valid method, at least in her opinion.

A final possible reading here is that "native speaker" framing was at the heart of all the decisions that were made. My decision to initiate pair- and group-work was done on the basis that I "knew" these were the correct approaches to language teaching. I did not seek the input of the students, and so my decision to do this could very well be seen as an imposition of Western methodological approaches on the class. However, my co-worker and the school owner can be seen as indulging another aspect of the ideology by insisting that my class focus on propagating "native speaker" norms of English, and thus placing me at the centre of the class. Once again, however, the students were not consulted. Seen from this angle, the incident can be read as two different forms of "native speaker" framing coming into conflict; methodological approaches clashing with the idealised model of the "native speaker" teacher. None of those involved seemingly felt it important to get the opinions of the students, and simply operated on normative assumptions about what was "best" for them. This incident highlights the complexity and contradictions of 'native speaker' framing. If these beliefs were objective and accurate reflections of the world, we could expect them to be coherent and harmonious. The fact that different aspects of the frame can come into conflict in this way simply indicates the extent to which it is an ideological filter, rather than a representation of objective reality.

Conclusion

In this chapter I have provided some short autobiographical vignettes from my time as an eikaiwa teacher, each selected in order to highlight certain discourses that I believe are implicated in the creation and promotion of the "native speaker" frame. As shown in the analysis, these discourses can be subtle, marginal and apparently unremarkable. However, when viewed through a critical lens their true ideological nature can be discerned. This is particularly true when aspects of the frame come into conflict, as in the final vignette. What all of these examples have in common, I have realised, is the lack of dialogue taking place with the students. Each vignette features teachers or school owners operating on *assumptions* of what is best for the students, based on their dominant perceptual frame. I hope this chapter may help teachers in eikaiwa to think critically about their experiences, and about how these experiences may be framed and filtered through a "native speaker"-centric worldview. Through this kind of reflexive critical thought, it may be possible to identify and challenge "native speaker" framing when we encounter it in our professional lives. While there may be numerous institutional, structural, and professional barriers that hinder our ability to challenge the "native speaker" frame, a greater awareness of our biases and skewed perceptions has the potential to lead us towards a place where all colleagues and students are treated with equal dignity and respect.

3. Just for the casuals? Leisure and learning in eikaiwa

Daniel Hooper

My time teaching at eikaiwa schools has had an indelible influence on my identity and continues to impact my development as a teaching professional. Over the course of my eight years as an eikaiwa teacher, I negotiated a range of different tensions both inside and outside of the classroom as I struggled to find my place as a professional teacher in environments where that was not always valued or even desired. In this chapter, I explore what was, for me, one of the most powerful of those tensions: a tension within the eikaiwa industry between education and entertainment.

One reason why I believe this distinction is an important one is that the idea of eikaiwa students being primarily there to learn language often seems to be taken as a commonsensical notion by English language teachers. At ELT conferences, I frequently heard the perspective of, "Of course eikaiwa students are motivated! They're paying for eikaiwa classes!" In response to these assumptions, I tried to describe how a considerable number of students that I had classes with often spoke largely in Japanese, didn't study at all outside of class, and appeared to be more interested in socialising with "native speaker"[2] English teachers (NESTs) or other students than in language acquisition. I wracked my brains for months over this perceived gap between what I was experiencing day in day out in class and what I was hearing "should be the case" from my peers.

It was at that time that I discovered an academic article that would open my eyes to the complexity of the eikaiwa experience and spark an interest in how eikaiwa is in some ways highly reflective of Japanese ELT at large. Kubota's (2011) article on eikaiwa schools explored the concept of learners being motivated by a plethora of factors including *akogare* (an eroticised or aspirational desire towards a foreign, and usually Caucasian, Other) and a desire to socialise with

[2] The words "native" or "native speaker" have been placed in quotation marks due to the recognition by the author that these terms are mere ideological constructions often on the basis of race, nationality, or physical appearance.

like-minded individuals. This phenomenon, to me, was far closer to what I was seeing in my workplace than the assumptions I was hearing from other academics.

A key element of this chapter is Kubota's questioning of the assumption that what goes on in eikaiwa always represents "linguistic and intellectual development" (p. 487) like language learning is perceived to be in more formal educational contexts. An alternative motivation for attending eikaiwa could be "casual leisure", a term coined by the sociologist, Robert A. Stebbins, who described a distinction between "serious leisure" (a deep interest in something resulting in a leisure career based on the pursuit of knowledge, skills, and experience in that area) and "casual leisure" (a relatively short-term activity solely for pleasure that requires little to no training) (Stebbins, 2007). Kubota argued that rather than an instrumental product resulting from classes, i.e. language acquisition, being primary, the eikaiwa students she interviewed found the pure enjoyment of engaging in eikaiwa to be the stimulus for attending classes. Although Kubota's article was groundbreaking for me, heavily influencing my perspective on eikaiwa classes, I was also wary of generalising her findings to all eikaiwa students. For every student I saw as seeking "casual leisure," there was another who I observed investing substantial time and effort into improving their English ability – the reality of eikaiwa was, of course, more nuanced and complex. Over time, I became more and more interested in the conflicting influences on teaching practice from learners seeking entertainment via "casual leisure" versus those pursuing development as part of their leisure career (Stebbins, 2007). These student demands, along with institutional pressure from eikaiwa schools for teachers to inhabit certain performative identities such as host or entertainer, were factors that markedly shaped my professional identity. In this chapter, I discuss the tension between entertainment and education, the ways in which it relates to both students and teachers, and how these ideas permeate all levels of ELT in Japan rather than being solely restricted to the eikaiwa classroom.

Eikaiwa students – casual or serious?

Kubota's (2011) article resonated with me as it gave a name to the phenomena I was frequently encountering in eikaiwa. Also tied to the notion of students as consumers of "casual leisure", Kubota discussed the idea of eikaiwa students as being motivated in part by *akogare* (longing/desire) towards Caucasian men and the exotic imagined community of "native" English speakers that they represent. I also experienced a number of key incidents that led me to believe in the potential role of the *akogare* Kubota described in the running and promotion of eikaiwa schools. One such incident occurred just as I had started my MA TESOL and contributed to the growing interest I had in eikaiwa schools' role in Japanese society. In my capacity as head teacher at a small eikaiwa school, I had hired a young teacher who had just completed his MA TESOL at a prestigious institution in the United States. He was an extremely competent teacher and influenced me a great deal in developing my own career. When his profile card was put up on the wall in the school's reception area, there was absolutely no mention made of his professional qualifications or experience. Rather than highlighting his competence as a teacher, the school chose to highlight how *oshare* (stylish) and smartly dressed he was. Later, the same school hired a young, blond, blue-eyed Caucasian British male teacher (with no qualifications or teaching experience) and immediately proceeded to create an advertising campaign in the local newspapers that I perceived to be centred primarily on his image as an idealised foreigner. Several locally distributed pamphlets were plastered with images of this young teacher posing and winking for the camera – information on his teaching beliefs or approach were notably absent. At this point in my tenure at eikaiwa, I became more and more pessimistic about the purpose of this school and the rationale of the students that attended their classes.

At this low point in my career, I was fortunate enough to have had a new student called Haruka (pseudonym) in one of my evening classes. Haruka had an extremely positive and outgoing personality and constantly looked for new ways to improve her English, using smartphone apps, doing extensive reading, and writing an English diary. Haruka's diary entries eventually became the focus of a case study (Hooper, 2019b) focusing particularly on her motivation for language learning as I felt that she represented such an unusual case in eikaiwa. Insights and reflections from her diary entries would in fact come to play a role in shifting the way in which I viewed *akogare* and the role of entertainment or fun in language learning. Haruka would often refer to how important it was for her to have fun in her classes. She said that if her classes had not been entertaining, then she would not have been able to maintain her motivation for study over such an extended period of time.

> At first I think that it is important that oneself enjoys study English. It is because I can't continue it if it isn't fun. (Hooper, 2019a, p. 30)

She also frequently indicated a sense of *akogare* towards an imagined community that she was intensely invested in: Hawaiian cultural experts. Haruka was a part-time hula and Tahitian dance teacher and Hawaiian culture certainly represented a "leisure career" for her with its influence bleeding into almost every facet of her life. English in many ways facilitated greater integration into that community as Haruka told me that she was now more able to communicate with her English-speaking hula teacher, and that her increasing English proficiency had aided her in her study of the Hawaiian language.

Through her case study and our conversations about her time as an eikaiwa student, Haruka taught me two important lessons. The first was that eikaiwa can become a site for "serious leisure" but also that fun or entertainment does not have to be divorced from learning. Haruka wrote a diary entry almost every day in English for a year, on top of reading graded readers and studying high-frequency word lists with no institutional requirement whatsoever to do so. Even now, when my university students are compelled to study in order to pass a course, I have yet to see a similar level of self-directedness and commitment to learning. The second lesson I learned was that *akogare* does not have to represent a sexualised desire or one tied to a narrow, problematic racial hierarchy with Western Caucasians positioned at the summit (Bailey, 2007; Kelsky, 2001). Nonaka (2018) also reconceptualised the concept of *akogare* and has reframed it in a far more facilitative light describing it simply as something "tantalizingly out of reach" (p. 3) that has the potential to greatly motivate language learners.

Through my experiences with Haruka, I was able to develop a more nuanced take on what I had learned from Kubota's paper and the utility of entertainment as a motivational tool in the classroom. Conversely, unresolved tension remained over the role entertainment played in shaping my professional identity as a teacher in eikaiwa and beyond.

> they (the eikaiwa school) encouraged teachers to be very energetic, outgoing, and even a bit clownish. While the company did not outright say it, they expected you to be an entertainer as well as a teacher. (Nuske, 2014, p. 118)

From my positionality as a NEST, this recount from Nuske's (2014) study into teacher resistance at an eikaiwa school resonated deeply with me. Just as with the school's reliance on *akogare* to attract new clients, I regularly observed incidences where I perceived eikaiwa schools to be framing the role of NESTs as entertainers or "hosts" (Kubota, 2011a) rather than educators. This was reflected in the hiring policies of the school I encountered as a head teacher where educational qualifications or experience appeared to be deemphasised in favour of traits such as youth, attractiveness, "*genki*ness" (how energetic or outgoing they were), or race. This tokenistic framing of the NEST role in eikaiwa has been documented in a number of studies (Kubota, 2011a; Nuske, 2014; Seargeant, 2009) and, as I will address in more detail later, also arguably permeates every level of English education in Japan.

How I perceived NESTs to be positioned within eikaiwa became a constant thorn in my side. At times, I used to (rather cynically) view my classes as being akin to a rollercoaster or a horror movie for some of my students: an anxiety-tinged but stimulating experience that they could step out of after a limited time and return to the safety of their regular lives unscathed. In fact, this idea may not be as far-fetched as one might think as can be observed through Kubota's (2011) description of an experience she had during data collection: "*As a sales-woman at a franchised eikaiwa gakkou in Tokyo who gave me a quick tour of tutorial cubicles said to me, 'It's so rare to sit so closely with a foreigner, isn't it?'*" (p. 486).

As I became more interested in teachers' professional identities and roles where I was working, I grew curious about how the eikaiwa experience compared to that of teachers working in a formal educational setting. This led me to initiate an exploratory research project investigating the lived experiences of eleven teachers (both Japanese and NESTs) who after teaching in eikaiwa, eventually transitioned into university teaching (Hooper, 2019a). While describing their professional role in both settings, a theme that emerged from many of the NEST interviews conducted (and that was not raised by my Japanese participants), was a difference between acting as an entertainer in eikaiwa and an administrator in university.

> But at eikaiwa, I think you're not seen as "*sensei*," to use the Japanese word. You're seen as just a guy or girl who's there to entertain them. (Hooper, 2019a, p. 9)

Several of the NESTs I spoke to also highlighted a distinction that they perceived between the "students" that they taught in university and the "customers" that they came into contact with in eikaiwa. The "student"/ "customer" distinction was in turn linked to the relative authority the teacher was afforded in each scenario. Therefore, these two themes taken together suggest that an ascribed identity of NEST entertainer in eikaiwa may have been conflated with a lack of authority and an eroded sense of professional identity. That being said, the majority of participants stated that there were many elements of their eikaiwa teaching including the closeness and reduced power differential that existed between teacher and learner that they still believed were very effective. Therefore, I learned that the lower formality that existed in my eikaiwa classes could be perceived as a double-edged sword. While representing a threat to teachers' self-identity as an education professional by pigeonholing them into a reductive 'entertainer' role, the reduced social distance in eikaiwa meant that a more egalitarian classroom and deeper teacher-learner bonds could be fostered.

Up until this point in my teaching career, I had largely only been exposed to NEST perspectives on eikaiwa either first hand from my colleagues or through the majority of existent research on the topic. Fortunately, this was to change with an opportunity to engage in a trioethnographic study with two Japanese eikaiwa teachers, Aya and Momoko (Hooper, Oka, & Yamazawa, 2020). In this study, using a grounded theory approach we were able to juxtapose our varied perspectives on eikaiwa teaching resulting in a more nuanced take on the industry that challenged our "common sense" assumptions. By exposing ourselves to perspectives not in line with our own, we all emerged from the study with many of our previous beliefs called into question. My co-researchers' experiences and the ways in which they described their NEST colleagues both confirmed and challenged assumptions that I had internalised from my subjective experiences and the literature on eikaiwa I had been exposed to. At times, they confirmed my beliefs about the tokenistic and trivialised image of "native speaker" eikaiwa teachers by describing them as "mascots" and questioning their classroom management skills.

> NESTs (native English speaker teachers) are like the mascots in an exciting theme park filled with special performances and exotic culture and fundamentally removed from reality. (Aya)

Conversely, Momoko and Aya actually painted a very different picture of student-teacher relationships in their schools to my eikaiwa experiences describing NESTs successfully inhabiting an authoritative teacher role.

> My experience is completely different from yours, Dan. My school provides loads of homework to students, both adults and young learners. We (both Japanese and foreign teachers) are entitled to check their homework every week and can be demanding if they haven't done it. Otherwise we believe they are not getting what they have paid for and that is not a good service. (Momoko)

These discussions with my co-researchers Momoko and Aya led me to question the idea of discussing eikaiwa as one uniform context with a defined set of characteristics. Both our trioethnography and Makino's (2016) "taxonomy of eikaiwa" clearly problematised the notion of eikaiwa as a monolithic entity, highlighting the vast scale of the industry and the huge range of diverse schools and individual teachers and learners it encompasses.

Not just for casuals? Eikaiwa as a microcosm of Japanese ELT

Although our trioethnography forced me to call into question many essentialised beliefs I harboured regarding eikaiwa NESTs and the eikaiwa industry as a whole, I felt the study revealed again the existence of certain trends related to the relationship between entertainment and eikaiwa teachers' professional identity. Furthermore, through reading more widely on ELT in Asia, I came to find that they were by no means limited to eikaiwa schools or even Japan.

Something linked to an ascribed identity (an identity assigned to an individual/group by others) of "entertainer" for NESTs in eikaiwa is an argument by Rivers (2013) that "native speaker" teachers in Japan are located in a "bounded space" – a performative identity ascribed by a sociocultural majority inhabited willingly or otherwise. In Rivers' study of teacher narratives, he showed that even in a formal university setting, the "native speaker" teacher could still be "cast as an innate entertainer" and that this role was "what many students and institutions have come to expect" (p. 49). Rivers' concept of a bounded space was echoed in an ethnographic study by Stanley (2013) of "native speaker" teachers in a private university in Shanghai. The way in which "fun" was constructed as a central component of these teachers' classroom role was explored in detail. Stanley described the bounded area in which teachers were positioned through the metaphor of a "clearing in the woods" (p. 160) – a demarcated space where teachers may negotiate a range of different but essentially limited identities. In this study, arguably parallel to eikaiwa, we see teachers' classroom efficacy judged primarily by the students and defined in terms of how closely their practice corresponded with the constructed image of an entertaining "native speaker" lesson. Stanley explained how, due to pressure from their institution/students who already have a socially constructed image of what a "native speaker" should be, NESTs may need to (willingly or otherwise) adopt the identity of the "fun" teacher. This can then be taken as reconfirming evidence by the institution/students that NESTs are indeed "fun" – and thus the cycle continues.

Of course, this is not to say that "native speaker" teachers in ELT are not the beneficiaries of significant privilege – they most certainly are, compared with both non-Japanese teachers defined as "non-native speakers" and many Japanese English teachers. However, within certain educational settings like eikaiwa I believe that we cannot accurately describe teachers' lived experiences in such simplistic terms. Nuske (2014) also recognised the complexity of the professional situation of "native speaker" teachers in eikaiwa as he has quite rightly described them as existing in "fluctuating systems of privilege and marginalization" (p. 126).

Nagatomo (2016) has also painted an evolving picture of Japanese ELT where formal educational settings like universities now represent "a buyer's market" (p. 50) due to increasing commercialisation stemming from a gradually shrinking student populace. In a similar vein to eikaiwa schools, universities are utilising images of Caucasian teachers in order to create a vibrant, international image as a selling point. Furthermore, these changes have meant a blurring between the positions of "student" and "customer." Consequently, teachers can feel pressured to teach "fun" classes in order to receive favourable student evaluations and thus increase their chances of long-term employment (Burrows, 2007).

I believe that although the trends described above are widespread throughout Japanese ELT, eikaiwa represents a microcosm of the whole where they are distilled and concentrated due to the primary motivation for eikaiwa schools being profit. Seargeant (2009) has emphasised eikaiwa's position as a site of tension within English teaching in Japan as he referred to it as the "most visible context in which the actualities of language learning within Japanese society clash with current trends and recommendations in contemporary TESOL theory" (p. 94).

So, where does all of this leave the NEST in eikaiwa (or beyond)? Are they powerless in the face of macro sociocultural and institutional pressures forcing them into a career of edutainment and unrelenting "*genki*ness," or do they possess total agency in moulding their own desired professional identity? I argue that, of course, neither is true. Canagarajah (1993) has argued that the classroom is somewhere in between unbending structural constraint and unrestrained agency, a site of "relative autonomy." Canagarajah's study, based on student domination and resistance in a Sri Lankan classroom, may seem distant from the struggle between entertainment and education in eikaiwa. However, I believe that his position on the "relative autonomy" of the classroom has something to teach NESTs in eikaiwa who are perhaps struggling with tensions over their identity. He claimed that students "are only partially free from the structures of domination in the larger social system" (p. 603), but that due to the diversity of cultures and beliefs in the classroom, a space can be created in which these structures can be questioned and resisted.

What I hope to express in this chapter is that the "relative autonomy" of the classroom could also apply to teachers (NEST or otherwise) in any level of Japanese ELT. When faced with threats to their professional identity or values, teachers have opportunities to engage in "position-taking", i.e. exercising agency through resistance to or reconstruction of one's assigned status, where they may "attempt to alter the patterns or practices of judgement in a social field" (Luke,

2009, p. 290). Additionally, from my own experiences, by building my professional skill set, becoming aware of the wider forces shaping my professional status while at the same time recognising the complexity of the classroom, I gradually became more comfortable in my own skin as I shaped a professional self while working in eikaiwa. In my classes, "fun" is a tool that I can employ when I judge it to be beneficial to learning, but I try not to let myself be defined by it. I strongly believe that by "position-taking" within the "relative autonomy" of the classroom, all ELT teachers both inside and outside eikaiwa can craft a fulfilling, professional version of ourselves that can serve our students well and that we can be comfortable with.

4. Foreign enough: Migrant nonnative English-speaking teachers in eikaiwa

Natasha Hashimoto

As a non-Japanese, nonnative English speaker teaching English in Japan, I am struck by the statement that "[t]here is something counterintuitive about migrant [nonnative] English teachers in non-English speaking countries other than their own" (Petric, 2009, p. 135) because that statement applies to many of us, migrant NNESTs employed outside our home countries. Although the dichotomising of native and nonnative speakers has been critiqued by scholars, many employers and learners continue to make this distinction, which is a big real life issue for many NNESTs. In Japan in particular, English language teachers are largely acknowledged as two prominent groups: native English speaking teachers (NESTs) from English-speaking countries and local, Japanese NNESTs. Non-Japanese NNESTs are seen as possessing neither group's perceived advantages, if any attention is paid to them at all. Unlike NESTs, they do not have English as their L1. Unlike Japanese NNESTs, they do not share their students' linguistic and cultural background. Thus, Poles or Mexicans, for example, teaching English in Japan might be seen as an oddity or even anomaly, or, more diplomatically put, nonmainstream. This socially constructed NES-NNES dichotomy continues to greatly affect many migrant NNESTs because employers prefer hiring NESTs (Braine, 2010), sometimes from only a handful of dominant English-speaking countries, rendering many qualified and experienced NNESTs unemployable.

However, although employers prefer hiring NESTs, many also hire Japanese NNESTs to teach beginners' classes or do administrative work (Hayes, 2013; Kubota, 2011a). Learners are thus perpetually exposed to very few types of English users – Japanese teachers of English and NESTs from a few countries, which might not be in the learners' best interest. Unlike some other languages that are arguably used more restrictively (e.g., Bulgarian to speak mainly with Bulgarians, Japanese almost exclusively for use in Japan), English has become a truly global language. More people speak it as a second or foreign language than as their first (Crystal, 2006). English language learners will also need to communicate in English with other NNESs in the future. Would they then not benefit from learning from a wider variety of teachers? That is what I have kept repeating to myself, in part trying to justify my own existence in ELT.

Becoming an eikaiwa teacher

I came to Japan as an accidental immigrant, after marrying a Japanese national overseas. I crossed borders without realising how greatly this transition would later affect my life (Kelley, 2013). I became an eikaiwa teacher accidentally, after looking for non-ELT work first. At that time, I had just returned from the United States where I had lived for several years, for the second time in my life, and earned a master's degree. I already had other qualifications such as a bachelor's degree from Japan and teaching credentials from the United States. I was multilingual, had work experience, and naively believed that I could build a career in Japan. Gradually, however, I realised that I could not find any job that would suit my educational background and earlier work experience. I then decided to try the eikaiwa industry, in spite of the low odds of being hired.

I found only a part-time job (20 work hours per week) in a small eikaiwa school, but even that job did not come to me easily. I was often unable even to apply or would be rejected before an interview because I did not fulfil the simple but fundamental requirements: I did not have a passport from an English-speaking country, was not a NES, and did not have 12 years of education in English. I probably did not seem "authentic" enough and lacked "a natural prestige" of NESs and the accompanying ability to represent the "original cultural context" (Kramsch, 1998, p. 79) of the English language. To this day, job postings on *GaijinPot* continue to require job applicants to speak English as a mother tongue. Sometimes, specific accents, typically American or British, are necessary on top of that. Postings that require a passport from a handful of English-speaking countries are also noticeable (GaijinPot, n. d.).

To be fair, rejection of foreign NNESTs is not unique to eikaiwa. An online search or a visit to any of the Japan-based TESOL conferences reveals that in Japanese universities, foreign NNESTs are nearly non-existent. Full-time and tenured foreign faculty tend to be NESs, even in departments devoted to teaching English as a Lingua Franca and World Englishes. If hired at all, foreign NNESTs tend to be contracted part-timers.

To my surprise, when I received an eikaiwa job offer, the Japanese employers wanted to hire me not only because of my teaching credentials but also for my Japanese language proficiency! They wanted to provide Japanese lessons taught by fluent non-Japanese, in addition to the courses taught by Japanese teachers. Just as they wanted their learners of English to study with diverse teachers, the employers wanted Japanese language learners to learn from both Japanese and non-Japanese teachers. Unfortunately, this job turned out to be a series of negative experiences for me (e.g., I received lower pay than my NEST colleagues). On the other hand, the job paid the bills and I enjoyed interacting with motivated adult learners.

Researching eikaiwa

Working in eikaiwa and being a doctoral student at the same time, I became interested in researching how other teachers perceived their jobs. I have interviewed close to 40 eikaiwa teachers and managers to date. The research participants are a diverse group of people but are mainly non-Japanese NNESs and NESs of Asian descent. I started interviewing them in 2013 for my still ongoing doctoral dissertation research. Most of these participants have experienced rejection due to their nationality, NNES status, or race. In this chapter, I share some of these teachers' stories, with their permission.

I found that in different contexts various individuals and groups both challenge and acknowledge these teachers' identities as legitimate English users. Furthermore, even though the NES participants of Asian descent are all from the Inner Circle and English is their L1, they are frequently misidentified as NNESs. Likewise, in some instances, White NNESTs' identity is obscured or ignored as these teachers are perceived as random foreigners (*gaijin*) and labelled, paradoxically, "native" only because of their phenotype. This oftentimes happens for marketing purposes only and some employers even instruct NNESTs to pretend to be NESs.

From reading a number of TESOL studies, I learned that due to rather normative expectations of how English teachers should look, speak, and where they should be from (elaborated in Kubota, 2011a and Seargeant, 2009), NNESs and people of colour seem undesirable in many ELT contexts. However, even though their NNES status and race were frequently perceived as liabilities, the accounts of the teachers I interviewed indicate that this matter is more complex. These teachers have had much to offer their students and this is sometimes recognised by employers and learners. Thus, the same teachers can be either privileged or marginalised in different settings, depending on gatekeepers' perceptions, needs, and even changing ideologies.

Workplaces and hiring practices

Eikaiwa is primarily a service industry. Therefore, emotional labour is intertwined with teachers' work as teachers are expected to build friendly relationships with students and provide a relaxing environment. Emotional labour refers to employees being pressured to control their feelings at all times. It requires workers to either suppress or evoke emotions and act as in ways that keep employers and clients satisfied. Focusing solely and excessively on meeting others' emotional needs can negatively impact on the worker's own emotional well-being and result in depression and burnout (for further details see, for example, Hochschild, 1983 and Tsang, 2019).

Many of the participants mentioned issues related to emotional labour. Luna (my study participant from Central Europe) reported that at her eikaiwa workplace teachers are required "to create a welcoming, friendly, open atmosphere to create a bond between the students and the school" so that they are satisfied and continue attending. Kate's (from Southeast Asia) former supervisors were strict and "pushed" the teachers to deliver relaxing lessons: "we can't use words like 'grammar.' That scares students ((laughter)). Or, '*read* this'—instead, we must say '*look* at this.'" The goal is to help learners relax and to avoid reminding them of conventional classrooms. To enforce such policies and "feelings and expression rules" (Tsang, 2019, p. 24), supervisors directly visit the classroom or control teachers via audio monitoring systems installed in classrooms.

Naturally, employers carefully choose whom to hire. A NES manager said that his former workplace hired both NESTs and NNESTs but:

> the management wanted young, lively, happy instructors. Mainly, teachers would get hired just because they can speak English. But, their personality and being fun was very important. Students were looking for a fun experience getaway, entertainment. Or, even therapy! We picked teachers that matched the school atmosphere.

Kate's experience with the eikaiwa job that she recently found is similar:

> They don't rate you based on your English but on your *genkiness [enthusiasm]*! It's all about your *yaruki [drive]*, your being *genki [energetic]*. Even during the breaks you are expected to talk to the customers. You're supposed to be outgoing, open. There are no real lessons, there's lots of shouting in English. You just show that you are *genki*.

The pressure to be fun and entertaining seems to affect both NESTs and foreign NNESTs equally. As long as they perform their "*genki*" foreigner roles, there is a place for a few NNESTs in eikaiwa schools. However, although having a suitable personality can secure jobs for teachers regardless of their first language and qualifications, NNES status is frequently a liability and many NNESTs find only part-time work.

Aware of limited employment opportunities, the participants apply for jobs cautiously. Kate said, "I look at the teachers' profiles on schools' websites. If I see teachers from [my country], I apply." I have always done something similar to that – I check if there are any other foreign NNESTs working where I consider applying for work. However, desperate for work, Dana (from Southeastern Europe) sometimes ignored the NES requirement. Employers "never responded because I'm from [a small European country], even though I have qualifications and experience."

A Canadian manager in my study insisted that "only people who speak like me [with a NES pronunciation] should be hired." His American colleague was even more uncompromising and would "never hire NNESTs," regardless of their credentials and skills. The NNESTs in the current study knew that by applying to these particular workplaces they would risk immediate rejection. Therefore, they applied for work selectively and chose only schools that seemed open to hiring NNESs.

The teachers in my study were powerless to contest this ascribed second-class NNES status when the definition of "NEST" meant having a passport from a certain country. All of the participants knew about these requirements. Negotiations of eligibility did not usually occur face-to-face, but the participants knew about the NEST requirement from advertisements, rejections, and their friends' experiences.

Acceptance of migrant NNESTs

Despite this general trend, some employers want to expose learners to diverse teachers and English varieties and employ teachers from many different countries, and they actively advertise this teacher diversity. Furthermore, some employers appreciate teachers' expertise in disciplines relevant to their clients' needs (e.g., experience in interpreting or business). Some recruiters said that many NNEST applicants were well-educated and spoke more than two languages. One recruiter shared that the NNESTs he hired are outstanding, knowledgeable teachers who connect with learners and that "only their accent gives away" their NNES status.

For Luna and Dana, receiving education in English-speaking countries meant that they could assume a new, expert English user identity. They were seen as legitimate teachers because people around them thought that living in "authentic" English-speaking countries made Luna and Dana seem more NES-like (also, see Lowe, this volume, for a discussion of native speaker framing). "Employers like to see such information in a CV," said Dana. I have also always disclosed my degrees from American institutions, hoping to be recognised as a legitimate English teacher in my students' and potential employers' eyes. The teachers who did not study in English-speaking countries, accordingly, reported that they did not like disclosing that fact to their students.

Although "a lot of research [suggests] that students prefer NESTs" (Galloway, 2014, p. 6), there is also evidence to the contrary (Llurda, 2015). One manager shared with me that at his school with over 20, mainly NES, teachers, "teachers from Singapore and Germany were very popular, and their lessons always fully booked." These particular teachers had graduate degrees and non-ELT professional expertise that matched their learners' needs.

However, even well-educated NNESTs' salaries were often the same or lower than those of NESTs without graduate degrees. This finding did not surprise me. When I worked in an eikaiwa school, a young NEST with a bachelor's degree took over a business English group lesson I had taught. He was paid 20 percent more than I was paid for teaching the same lesson. When he quit a few months later, I was asked to teach the same lesson again but for my original, lower pay!

White and foreign enough to be hired

The participants of my study reported frequently feeling marginalised and discriminated against. Kate (Southeast Asian) mentioned a job interviewer's words: "We prefer native speakers. They meant White! Or, Black maybe," but not Asian; "*Ideally*, you'd be American, Canadian. On Craigslist, [some employers] specify teachers' gender, nationality, and Whiteness." She concluded that her male NES acquaintances can be "picky" about eikaiwa jobs that they can "easily find."

Some NNESTs hide their nonnative status from learners because employers instruct them to (Galloway, 2014). Ella (Africa) resented that her employers "always asked me to pretend to be a NES. They always lied to the students and parents [that I'm a NES]." None of the 10 managers I interviewed, however, reported that their workplaces required that such an act be put on by NNESTs.

Luna mentioned how her "young, cheerful, American friend who teaches children" and whom "the school can successfully market" is paid significantly more than a Filipina coworker doing "exactly the same job." She then added: "Japanese mainly think [people of my nationality] are trustworthy, professional, diligent, punctual, so I'm actually perceived positively. I'm also labeled White." Ella mentioned "a British recruiter" who was "glad I'm a White [African] because [students'] parents don't really like Black teachers. [Being White] definitely made it easier to get hired because some people explicitly say they like teachers who *really* look foreign—tall and blonde."

Some teachers, like me, grew up in, arguably, historically less heterogeneous, very small European countries. We felt that we *became* White in Japan. We became a visible (due to our phenotype) minority because our skin colour has become a marked aspect of our identity. Ivan (Central Europe) is of partial Japanese descent but believes that "if you're not 100 percent pure Japanese, you're *not* Japanese!" For him, this translates into being able to find ELT work: "I wasn't always rejected when I applied" to places that wanted only NESTs. For various reasons, some of the participants in my study were perceived as White enough and foreign enough to be hired, just like the participants in Petric's (2009) and Galloway's (2014) studies, despite being NNESTs.

Some, like Kate, readily assumed this "foreign enough" identity whenever given a chance to do so. She also purposely adopted an appropriate accent. For this, she is sometimes criticised:

> My friends from non-English-speaking countries always give me a hard time for my accent. "Why do you speak English like an American, where's your identity?" But, back home, I don't speak like this, I use [my L1] accent. I speak like this *in Japan*.

Kate simply used her "American accent" at work because of its market value, similar to how Galloway's (2014) Eastern European NNEST was rewarded for using an "American accent" in Japan.

Many NNESTs, however, are unable to acquire native-like English accents. Unfortunately for us, many types of foreign English accents are perceived negatively (Lippi-Green, 2012) and NNESTs are mocked because of our accents. Jokes about accents continue to be acceptable in many circles. Furthermore, from personal experience and from the interviews with the research participants, it is evident that the "problem" with foreign accents is regularly brought up in job interviews and scepticism toward non-native English accents is openly expressed.

Marketable assets

Diverse international and educational backgrounds, relevant work experience, and multilingualism are the participants' marketable assets or cultural capital (see Bourdieu, 1986, for a discussion on various types of capital) that can be converted to economic gains. Luna and Dana studied in English-speaking countries, which is an added value. Kate worked in several different countries in Asia and Europe; this experience is useful when she teaches business English as she can confidently discuss different corporate cultures. Ivan reported:

> I try to bring in a European perspective. I've been to many European countries, and I try to talk about that. I see this as a strength definitely because my students are happy with what I teach and with the perspective I provide, as a [European, and] NNES.

Ella, who owns a business, tells her students about her experience living in another Asian country and doing business globally. She also appreciates the opportunity to teach about her culture:

> As a NNES and because I have my own, [African] culture, I can contribute a bit more with teaching about it. Although I know those other [English-speaking] cultures—we're exposed to British and American culture in [my country] through media and education—I can also contribute with my own [culture and] accent.

Some other participants also introduced their countries and cultures to interested students and felt that their contribution extended beyond ELT. They had something additional they could share and mostly saw this aspect of their identity in a positive light.

Each participant's particular educational background and work experience outside teaching were also relevant to their eikaiwa jobs. Experience or credentials in education were evaluated particularly positively. Dana believed that her studying pedagogy and languages made her employable. Ivan had taught a university course in his home country, which is an added bonus because some employers need teachers with teaching experience. Grace's employer appreciated her work experience with childcare in her home country, so she has continued working with children for over ten years in the same school in Japan.

Other work experiences and education, seemingly unrelated to pedagogy and English, are also sometimes in demand. For example, Ivan's work experience in consulting and Luna's in media-related jobs were also important in their business English teaching in their eikaiwa schools:

> My business background gave me more access to different [ELT] jobs because many of them require a business background, to teach business related topics to business people. This business experience is more valued by employers because it's probably rarer than having teaching experience alone. (Ivan)

Multilingualism is also appreciated sometimes (most of the participants speak at least three languages). Dana has studied Italian, German, Spanish, and is fluent in Japanese, which her employers valued. Although her L1 was never in demand, Dana sometimes taught children Italian in her school and was pleased with that. Kate, fluent in French, sometimes provided French conversation opportunities for Japanese learners of French at her workplace where various languages are taught. Ella had the chance to teach Mandarin, and Luna has taught her L1 (a major European language) in the past. As a multilingual, I also share my participants' belief that our multilingualism makes us good language teachers because we have developed a deep metalinguistic awareness.

The narratives shared above indicate that in environments accepting of NNESs, the participants thrive as teachers while educating students in their respective fields of expertise. They can bring in perspectives different from those of dominant English-speaking countries and contribute their own cultural, professional, and linguistic diversity.

Professional teacher identity?

The participants in my study avoided calling themselves teachers. Instead, they emphasised their role as facilitators who share their English knowledge and professional expertise. They also saw their ELT jobs as temporary. Unstable eikaiwa jobs (mostly part-time jobs, short-term contracts without benefits), a NNES status, feeling inadequate, and lack of career development might be obstacles to fully developing a career and a professional teacher identity. The participants do not have much opportunity for professional development in their workplaces and are not required or encouraged to gain knowledge of pedagogy. Their employers do not seem to be equipped to evaluate such skills and credentials. An Australian NEST/manager described the situation of many other (NES and NNES) eikaiwa teachers he worked with. This excerpt might best summarise some of the NNESTs' participants' sentiment as well:

> There are many teaching techniques, a lot of theory behind teaching, which we don't know about. I wouldn't really call myself a teacher. I don't teach the language… I think it's maybe facilitating… we do more of that. So, I wouldn't say I'm actually a teacher.

He might have just been humble, however, because as I interviewed him over the span of six years, I saw that he had plenty of varied teaching experience and a plethora of ideas about how to engage the learner.

However, it might also be that some participants simply chose jobs (i.e., working in order to earn money), not necessarily careers (i.e., a more fulfilling endeavour that involves professional development). Braine (2010) posed a question about the issue of whether NNESTs "teach English more as a means of livelihood than as a calling" (p. 41). Although I do not argue that this choice pertains only to NNESTs, it seems that for many, eikaiwa work is a job that pays the bills, not a career that fulfils and allows personal growth. To illustrate, I quote Grace, who explained how she started teaching:

> I didn't speak Japanese back then [and] the only thing I could do and I kind of liked doing was teaching kids English. This job is always easy to get because there's a constant need for teachers. They leave because teaching children is hard work. Parents do want good English from teachers, but they also want a gentle, experienced teacher who can teach children some kind of discipline. That's more important to them because I spend 20 hours a week with their child.

When speaking about the limitations of making their jobs a career, Ivan commented on the "exploitative system" of the commercial sector where teachers are "at the bottom" of the hierarchy. Kate had a similar opinion:

> [Eikaiwa] is a dead-end job. Some become managers, but what else? You'll be teaching, teaching, teaching, sometimes 10-12 lessons daily [to make a living], follow that lesson checklist, and you can't even make much money. We get just 2 yen raise [per lesson every year], *if* we're evaluated well!

Kate considered herself fortunate to have a spouse with a regular job, and together they could make a living. She cannot see eikaiwa as a context in which to build a career.

Most of the participants plan to leave eikaiwa and find more stable, fulfilling careers. Some have already left. Grace, older than the other participants, is aware of the lack of choices and continues working. She is "lucky I don't have children. I [must] take care only of myself, and I can survive in any situation. Teaching children, I can always make enough money to survive."

With irregular employment, lack of benefits and professional development opportunities, and wages that rarely rise despite qualifications and experience, it is understandable that teachers cannot build careers and fully develop a professional teacher identity. However, many of them still enjoy connecting with their students and teaching. Despite feeling insecure about unstable employment, they try to contribute with their expertise while they are still working in the industry.

Conclusion

In this chapter I discussed the complexities of NNESTs' eikaiwa work. Although migrant NNESTs still appear marginalised, certain cultural capital (Bourdieu, 1986) such as particular professional experience and educational background allows some of them to be accepted in a context which has traditionally treated a NNES status as a liability. Despite challenges, the teachers I interviewed presented themselves as educated, experienced, globally-oriented, proficient English users. They did not identify as conventional ELT professionals in traditional educational institutions, but they were experts in many ways: expert English language users, educated in their disciplines, and experienced learning facilitators who share their expertise with their students. However, the teachers believed that their time in the industry was limited and felt that they had to find other work due to the lack of both full-time jobs and support for professional development from their employers. The time to leave for most of them seemed to be approaching fast.

For some of us, that time has long passed. I was fortunate not to spend too many years in the particular eikaiwa school that I worked for. I confess that, although I enjoyed interacting with my adult students and made a few good friends with my colleagues, I might still be haunted by my own eikaiwa experience. It was disheartening to see how little positive effect my teaching experience, positive student feedback, and my TESOL education had on my career. I was able to find only part-time work and my salary remained unchanged.

However, my eikaiwa experience has given me a venue to explore it as a research interest. The process helped me become a critical researcher and find a group of like-minded TESOL scholars to collaborate with, for which I am grateful. I am also thankful to the research participants for sharing the stories of their eikaiwa journeys with me. I heard my own past and present in their stories. I truly hope that our futures will see us as more than simply "good enough" for the job.

5. Japan has four seasons: *Nihonjinron* and native-speakerisms at the *eikaiwa gakkou*

Martin Cater

I came to Japan from the UK in late 2004 after securing my first English teaching job at one of the large eikaiwa school chains, which are often referred to in academic literature as *eikaiwa gakkou* (Kuboto, 2011a). I was to stay at that company for just over ten years, the last five of which were spent as a Senior Teacher working exclusively at a branch located in central Tokyo. Before I left, I had completed a Diploma in TESOL and then an MA by distance, courses of study which afforded me the opportunity to conduct some academic research within the sector. This chapter discusses experiences I had leading up to that research and the circumstances surrounding it, contextualising the studies and my personal experiences within the limited eikaiwa literature and the wider body of work on native-speakerism.

A warm welcome

Looking back, my research interests within eikaiwa were shaped by encounters I had during the first couple of years at my company, before I had decided to fully commit to a career in teaching. They centred around two aspects: the perceived importance of the native-speaker status of English language teachers, and the Japanese learners' perceptions of themselves. I initially saw these aspects as distinct, but over time I came to see them as being fundamentally connected in some way.

Most people employed at my eikaiwa were recruited overseas, sourced largely from the UK but also Canada, Australia, New Zealand, and to a lesser extent, America. We were all regarded as "native speakers" – a term which, while impossible to satisfactorily define, was understood on a practical level by teachers, staff and students at the schools. For most instructors there, including myself, the eikaiwa chains were associated with two important firsts: our first experience of teaching English as a full-time job, and also the first time we had lived in a foreign country. A majority of us were therefore young, in our early to mid-twenties, and we were looking to explore a new part of the world. Fortunately, Japan proved to be a relatively easy country to reside in, despite the language-barrier; and the students were also very friendly and supportive. Being assigned to classes as a regular teacher enabled me to get to know my students as people in addition to their strengths and weaknesses in language. Although most lessons were designed to include some explicit grammar teaching, the focus was on conversation practice on specific topics using target language. This undoubtedly made the instruction easier for inexperienced teachers like me, and it also enabled us to learn about Japan through asking questions and listening to our students' opinions. In general, I found the students eager to talk to me about their country.

Japan has four seasons

It is fair to say that I learned a lot about Japan and the Japanese people from my students at the eikaiwa. I feel incredibly grateful to them for this. My memories of those early conversations are overwhelmingly positive, although I occasionally heard beliefs expressed that I found rather difficult to understand coming from my own British background. Those exchanges stood out for that reason; and, after speaking to colleagues, I discovered that many other teachers had participated in similar conversations where some of the same beliefs were communicated. It appeared that these ideas were widespread, and they had a slightly alienating effect on us.

My first encounter with what I would later discover was known as *nihonjinron*, a set of popular discourses on the supposed uniqueness of the Japanese language, culture, and race (Lie, 2004), was when I was told by a student that Japan has four seasons. This fact alone was not odd, but rather that I was informed that this was a 'unique' benefit of living in Japan. The student seemed to be quite proud of this. Initially I thought that the learner had misunderstood the meaning of the word "unique," so I tried to check that they understood it conceptually. I clearly remember referencing the world map on the wall of the classroom; what I found challenging was that the concept of uniqueness had actually been understood, but there seemed to be a disconnect when I pointed out that the passing of the seasons could be enjoyed in a great many countries. There was a reluctance to engage. I certainly didn't force the discussion, so we moved on and enjoyed the rest of the class.

Other examples of *nihonjinron* ideology that emerged in my classroom experience concerned the complexity of the Japanese language and the uniqueness of the Japanese body. On the former, some students commented that foreigners could not hope to speak like native Japanese because of Japanese people's understanding of the vagueness and complexity of the language. As with the four seasons, this appeared to be a source of pride for many. Regarding the body, I found that some students believed that the Japanese possess an intestine of greater length than those of the other peoples of the world, apparently due to the consumption of a vegetarian diet which took place over a number of centuries in the past. I also found that the fact that Japan is an archipelago which was largely closed off from the outside world between 1639 and 1853 was often used as a standard explanation to account for a wide range of phenomena, ranging from why some students felt the Japanese tended to be shy, to why Japanese people work longer hours in general than workers in many other developed countries.

A direct connection between *nihonjinron* and the *eikaiwa gakkou* has been highlighted in the literature. Seargeant (2009) describes how the Nova eikaiwa chain drew from pseudoscience originally propounded by Tsunoda (1978), a professor from the prestigious University of Tokyo, who claims that "Japanese brains" handle sound differently to "Western brains," postulating differences in the way vowel sounds are processed in the hemispheres. In 2005, the company ran an advert (in Seargeant, 2009, p. 97) stating that Japanese and English exist on "different wavelengths," and that "a normal Japanese person's brain cannot distinguish English… from noise." Fortunately, a solution was at hand: "to listen repeatedly to and speak with native speakers," who of course were readily available at the *eikaiwa gakkou* chains. I was one of them at the time the advert was published.

Professionalising at eikaiwa: A brief counter-narrative

After my first couple of years I noticed fewer instances of *nihonjinron* in the classroom. Part of the reason for this could have been that I had become so used to hearing it that such ideas had lost their novelty, but I think that it was also due to my interest in developing as a teacher: rather than asking my students questions about Japan, I was asking myself questions about my practice. I was certainly not the only one. Although most *eikaiwa gakkou* instructors did not stay at my company for more than two years, some continued; and almost all of that group consciously made unpretentious efforts to improve their practice. I found that I was steadily becoming more popular as a teacher, and I do not believe that this change had any connection with my appearance. I make this point because the scant literature on *eikaiwa gakkou* has often fetishised these schools as "eroticized locales" (Bailey, 2007) where Japanese women go in order to initiate sexual relationships with Caucasian males. This sentiment was also given prominence by Kubota (2011) in describing a conversation with the Japanese owner of an independent eikaiwa school. These were not environments that I recognised; and it seemed clear to me that my own popularity was based on my improving teaching competence. Adult students of all profiles were increasingly requesting my lessons. Working on the diploma was of particular significance to my creativity: I "flipped" my classrooms before I was aware of the concept in the literature; experimented with aspects of the Silent Way using the International Phonetic Alphabet; and incorporated soft data-driven learning into my classes, the latter of which I presented on at a national teaching conference (Cater, 2014). Seargeant (2009) has criticised eikaiwa for their use of standardised lesson plans as stifling examples of McDonaldization; they are, in my view, a necessary support for new teachers who have no classroom experience. My line manager actively encouraged creativity, provided that specific language points were covered and the students were satisfied with their lessons. I am particularly keen for the above points to be put on record in an academic context as I feel they run counter to a narrative which portrays *eikaiwa gakkou* teachers and students negatively in a way which is not entirely justified. I do not wish to be an apologist for an industry which undoubtedly has many problems, but some balance is both necessary and overdue.

The research project: Native-speakerisms, one or many?

Before I left my company, I was keen to gather data for a small research project on eikaiwa. I needed to do this as part of my university dissertation, but I also hoped that the finished work would be of sufficient quality to share with the academic community, offering something different to the existing eroticised narratives. As a theme, I was strongly drawn to the concept of native-speakerism (Holliday, 2005), not only because I found it interesting but also because I felt it was particularly recognisable in the *eikaiwa gakkou* context. Holliday described native-speakerism as a racist ideology whose upholders believe that native speakers of English are the ideal English teachers. People who subscribe to it feel this way because they believe that so-called "native" instructors are connected to Western culture and Western teaching methodologies in a way that non-native teachers are not. The heavy promotion of native speakers in the advertising material of the *eikaiwa gakkou* sector suggested the presence of the ideology and I wanted to discover whether the students held native-speakerist views. I also felt that there was possibly something more, however: in the essentialised image of the native-speaker English teacher described by Holliday, I saw a reflection of the perception of Japaneseness and a unique Japanese self which runs throughout *nihonjinron* discourses: the land; the language; the race. In my local Japanese context, I strongly suspected that a belief in the superiority of a native-speaker English teacher may be connected with these ideas, and in particular the belief that a non-native Japanese could never master the Japanese language. I wanted to explore this through my project, and designed a study that would test *eikaiwa gakkou* learner perceptions of native and non-native speaker teachers of English and Japanese.

In seeking to determine whether native-speakerism existed related to Japanese language teaching, I had to move away from Holliday's traditional model (2005), which is exclusively focused on ELT. Holliday has claimed that native-speakerism does not exist beyond the scope of English teaching, asserting that there is little evidence for it (2015). An alternative model has been proposed, however, which broadened the definition through a decoupling which allowed for its application to teachers of any language (Houghton & Rivers, 2013). I was therefore able to use the later model as a framework for my investigation into parallel native-speakerisms.

Results and further reflections on native-speakerism in Japan

I was successfully able to complete the research through the kind assistance of school counsellors at my branch, and presented the results at JALT national conferences in 2016 (Cater, 2017) and 2017 (Cater, 2018). In short, questionnaire findings suggest that the sample likely held native-speakerist views regarding ELT as data indicated that more respondents felt that native speakers were competent at teaching pronunciation, speaking, listening, reading, writing and grammar compared with results for both Japanese teachers of English and other non-native English speaker teacher alternatives. The most interesting part for me, however, was that when asked to imagine the teaching competencies of non-native Japanese instructors of the Japanese language in the same teaching areas, the bias towards the native speaker—in this case, Japanese—was even stronger. The fact that native-speakerism was evident in both languages with a bias towards the L1 suggests to me that the ideology might also be connected to learner perceptions surrounding their first language rather than being entirely a consequence of ELT marketing strategies and practices. Readers interested in the details of my study are advised to access the papers online, where they are freely available. Here, I will discuss some additional data related to the project that I was unable to include, which do not neatly fit into established academic thinking on the ideology.

In the Japanese *eikaiwa gakkou* context, students tend to be familiar with two types of instructors: Japanese teachers of English, and native-speaker English teachers. Teachers from countries other than the traditional homes of English are present in Japan, but they are not marketed in a specific category and therefore exist in a kind of grey area (Hashimoto, this volume). My company did occasionally employ these instructors—I worked with a very gifted teacher from Greece for a couple of years, for example—and as far as I am aware, no doubts were ever expressed as to whether they were regarded as equal to native speakers in terms of proficiency, by the students or any of the teachers I came into contact with. In relation to my study, because of the lack of awareness about them, I defined this non-native speaker teacher group separately on the questionnaire myself, gathering responses related to beliefs about them in a category distinct from Japanese teachers of English and native English speaker teachers. Unsurprisingly, when participants answered questions about this group, "don't know" responses were significantly higher than for the other two categories; however, the few individuals who recorded that they had been taught by such teachers at some point in their lives evaluated them positively.

I did not provide a description of what a native speaker was, instead asking participants to provide their own definition as an open response at the beginning of the form. I wanted to do this because many academics are keen to draw attention to semantic problems associated with the phrase (Lowe & Kiczkowiak, 2016); most put the word in inverted commas or quotation marks to emphasise that the term is fuzzy and lacking in objectivity. I intended to assess how diverse the eikaiwa students' perceptions of it were in my local context. The results indicated a great uniformity in that it was seen as synonymous with the Japanese phrase for "mother tongue speaker," as the clear majority of participants responded with this entry. A notable deviation from this was one of my own students in the pilot, who wrote "a person from America or the UK." I assume from this that the average student's understanding of the concept is analogous to that of a non-specialist from an inner circle country, where, like Japan, monolingualism is the norm. A teacher's skin colour was not given as a criterion by any of the respondents, despite the ubiquity of Caucasian models in online and print advertising.

I decided to include two Likert items on the topic of race, one of which specifically related to Caucasians, which were mixed in with statements on other areas of interest. The reason for doing so was because of the prominence of whiteness in the *eikaiwa gakkou* literature going back to Lummis (1976), the contemporary advertising referred to above, and a small number of troubling conversations I had had with School Counsellors and line managers concerning students who had asked to change instructor for reasons of race, explicitly or implicitly. The statements included on the form were as follows: "I would prefer to study English with a white teacher," and "I have no preference regarding the race of my instructor." I assumed that it was clear that the first of these statements was racist as one of my own students made a note on the form indicating this in the pilot, and I was therefore not expecting any responses in agreement with it in the sample. A male participant in the study aged 25 to 34 actually felt compelled to write "race is not important" next to the line on the form; however, to my dismay, of the sample of 32, two females – one aged between 18 and 24, and another aged over 65 – agreed with the former statement. The younger female also disagreed with the second, while the older participant chose the "don't know" option. It appears that racism continues to be a problem.

Epilogue

Looking back, I have many good memories of my time working within the *eikaiwa gakkou* sector, all of which are connected with the students I taught and the people I worked with. I feel pleased that I was able to complete a small project within the environment before I left, which offers a different perspective to what had been done before. I hope that others will look into native-speakerism related to student beliefs about the possibilities of foreigners mastering the learner's own language, as I suspect that, in some contexts, one of the roots of the ideology may lie there. *Nihonjinron* offers a particularly conspicuous example of linguistic and cultural nationalism, but it would be short-sighted to imagine that these beliefs are only evident in Japan.

On a practical level, I also felt that my project may have had a positive impact when it came to race and advertising in the short-term. After completing the study, I shared some of my concerns with the Teachers' Representative, asking him to tell management of the need to represent diversity to current and potential students. He communicated this to the principal, and it was reported on in the teachers' newsletter. The principal claimed that the lack of representation of non-white teachers in adverts had not been deliberate, and said that the company would look to take steps in the future. Shortly afterwards, a non-white female teacher was featured prominently throughout the company website and in sales literature. I don't know whether this change was made directly as a result of my intervention, but I felt that it was a positive move that would benefit everyone. I estimate that this female remained on the website for approximately two years while she was employed at the company. After she left, she was removed, however, to be replaced with a new assortment of Caucasian men in their twenties.

After leaving the *eikaiwa gakkou* but remaining in Japan, I still encounter native-speakerism and *nihonjinron* in the contexts of private teaching, examining, and working in the tertiary sector. The young adults I teach seem to be just as likely to subscribe to these ideologies as their parents' generation, suggesting that these concepts continue to be reinforced rather than challenged. While I do not think that it is reasonable to hold ELT businesses such as *eikaiwa gakkou* wholly responsible for perpetuating essentialised discourses, I feel they could do more to counter these ideas than they are at present. This is particularly important as these corporations have recently started expanding into Japanese universities: one of them is sending in instructors to teach credit-bearing courses at an institution I work at from 2020; and from conversations with colleagues, it appears that my university is not an isolated case. As a consequence of this shift, essentialised ways of thinking could become even more entrenched.

Part 2: Negotiating pedagogy

6. Developmentally appropriate practices vs. parental wishes: The eikaiwa owner's quandary

Lesley Ito

The father who sat across the table from me at the parent-teacher conference was very concerned about his eight-year-old daughter. "She still makes grammatical errors when she writes," he said. "Don't you teach her any grammar rules? That's how I learned English when I was in junior high school. How is she supposed to learn grammar if you don't teach her the rules?"

If that question had been posed to a regular elementary school teacher, the teacher could probably pull from the educational training they received in college and attempt to educate the parent about developmentally appropriate practices honestly and without fear of any consequences. However, answering that type of question as an eikaiwa teacher is fraught with risk. Many eikaiwa teachers or school owners might not have the educational training in child development that a typical elementary school teacher may possess and probably do not command the same level of respect. Furthermore, if the parent is dissatisfied with the answer, they may quit the school and enrol in another eikaiwa that prioritizes parent satisfaction over following developmentally appropriate teaching practices. This is even more of a difficult situation if the school is still starting out and there are financial pressures to keep or attract any students they can. School owners with perfectly good intentions to teach their students appropriately may feel pressure to compromise for the sake of building up their business.

It is hoped that parents always want what's best for their children. However, in my experience, it seems they often make decisions on their child's English education based on what they encountered as students or the advice of friends. Some parents may even base their decisions on rumors or information gleaned from self-styled "mama bloggers", who may not have any experience in education other than trying to raise their own child to be bilingual. Still others hope to raise a child prodigy and seek the bragging rights that come when their children pass a test designed for adults or pass some other benchmark at an unusually young age. (To give an example of this taken to the extreme, my own school has received occasional requests from parents with babies under one year old who believed their baby was a genius and should take part in my lesson for elementary school age students.)

Occasionally, parents will dismiss advice given by non-Japanese eikaiwa school owners, implying that as they received their education in another country, they couldn't possibly understand the Japanese educational system. This is compounded by the fact that many eikaiwa owners, despite having four-college degrees, do not have TESOL certification, as most start in entry-level eikaiwa positions that usually do not require any, before eventually deciding to open their own school. These teachers are sometimes still interested in furthering their professional development and may read books or attend teaching presentations, yet feel frustrated when parents might not readily respect explanations based on this knowledge.

When opening their own school, some school owners may feel they should follow the business owners' mantra of "the customer is always right" and adopt practices that are developmentally inappropriate because the parents of the young students request them to do so. Some of these owners may feel an internal struggle because they know such developmentally inappropriate practices might not be in the best interest of the child, but some school owners may not be aware of what child development experts suggest. Other schools with owners who understand more about child development cannot help but be influenced by these types of schools and may put aside what they know is right

As an eikaiwa school owner, I have done my best to offer a curriculum that is developmentally appropriate for children and have occasionally lost business because parents didn't understand the long-term benefits. However, in the long run, my belief in following pedagogically sound methods has led to increased enrolment and students who sometimes stay in the program for more than ten years. Being in the business for decades, getting an MSc in Teaching English to Young Learners (TEYL), and having a child who went through the Japanese school system and secured a place at Tokyo University, all contributed to parents trusting that my school's methods would be effective. However, it took a long time to get to this point and I still spend time counselling parents and explaining the reasons behind the curriculum to show that I had their child's best interests at heart.

In this chapter, I discuss pedagogical issues that parents are often concerned with. In particular, I cover the areas of teaching grammar to children, children using adult EFL textbooks, issues with writing, and children taking adult English tests. Anecdotes and experiences from my 25 plus years of teaching young learners will also be shared. Each section will begin with a paraphrased quote based on parental comments I have heard over the years.

Grammar

> *"Why does my son [8 years old] still write 'He do' instead of 'He does'? He's been learning English for two years now. By the time I was in the second year of junior high school, I had already mastered this rule."*

Experts on teaching children EFL have argued that children under the age of ten should not be taught grammar explicitly using meta-language (Cameron, 2001; Pinter, 2006). The best way to teach children grammar is through "rote learnt chunks" (Cameron, 2001, p. 104) encountered in songs, chants, or stories. However, many of the parents who send their children to eikaiwa schools may have learned English for the first time in junior high school. They learned English using traditional methods, such as being taught grammar rules explicitly using meta-language, and may not be aware that these methods are inappropriate for children. Mastering grammar rules is important to them and they fret over their children's grammar mistakes in homework or other writing assignments. This is especially upsetting to parents of returnee students, who may not understand why their children make careless grammar mistakes despite their high level of English fluency. When parents ask for help with their child's grammar, they often expect me to respond by giving them grammar worksheets to complete. It takes some convincing that a more effective method would be having their child read a book that interests them, in order to provide exposure to chunks of language and natural grammar patterns.

Another issue that parents might not be aware of is that some of their child's grammatical mistakes may be due to their current stage of development. Teachers and parents cannot expect a child to do something in their second language (L2) that they cannot yet do in their first (L1). I have reassured parents in the past by showing letters children wrote to President Obama when he was in office. These children were trying to do their best, writing letters in their L1 to an important person, yet they had a number of grammar, punctuation, and spelling errors. Such an example shows parents that it is unrealistic to expect a young child to produce writing that is error free. In fact, insistence on perfect writing may result in the child becoming less motivated to write or holding back their creativity because they fear making mistakes (Linse & Nunan, 2006).

As part of my MSc in TEYL studies, I conducted an action research project in my own school on error correction (Ito, 2019), and the results supported Cameron (2001) and Pinter's (2006) recommendations. When the top ten most common errors made by students were identified and brought to their attention, students over the age of ten were able to learn from this and not repeat those errors. Students under the age of ten, however, found the error correction to be frustrating and their errors did not decrease. Upon the conclusion of this project, an announcement was sent out to the parents of young students to let them know that teachers would no longer be making red pen corrections on certain writing assignments for students under the age of ten. While a few parents complained and expressed anxiety that their children would not learn correct grammar if red pen corrections were stopped, most of the parents were supportive and realized the decision was based on research.

While most experts in the field agree that young EFL students should not be taught grammar the same way adults are, there is actually very little recent research on teaching grammar or learning to self-correct errors with this age group (Amirian & Sadeghi, 2012).

Children using adult EFL textbooks

Parent: "So, this is the textbook my daughter used at her old school."
Teacher: "But. . .she's six years old, right? This is a textbook for adults."
Parent: "Oh, really?"

There have been two cases of children in the first or second grade of primary school revealing to me during the initial assessment all students interested in my school must go through that they had been taught using popular adult EFL textbooks at their former school. In one case, the child was a *kikokushijo*, a returnee student who had received her early education in English, and the other was a child who had graduated from an international pre-school. After asking why the child had using an EFL textbook for adults, I learned that it had been chosen by the former teacher. As I had no opportunity to ask the teacher their reasons for choosing such an inappropriate textbook for a young child, I can only speculate the teacher concluded that a child with such high-level English compared to their peers should be able to handle learning from an adult textbook, either due to teacher misunderstanding what appropriate materials would be for this type of student or out of desire to impress the parents. I have also had preschool students from a large educational chain school whose parents proudly claimed they could complete worksheets intended for junior high school students who come in for initial assessments. Despite their children's supposedly amazing grammatical feats, they were unable to read simple graded readers for young learners and could not answer basic questions such as, "What color is it?" or "How many _____ are there?"

Writing

> *"My three-year-old daughter can already write all of the ABCs and her name in English. Isn't this great?"*

Many parents in Japan seem to have the idea that "earlier is better" and a sign of a child's high intelligence. They do not understand why asking children to write before their fine motor skills have developed may not be a good idea. Children taught using the Montessori method are encouraged to use crayons to color, play with modelling clay, or use scissors to cut bits of paper in order to build up the muscles in their hands. Then they trace sandpaper letters with their fingers, trace letters with their fingers in fine sand, write on a chalkboard with a large piece of chalk, and finally use a moveable alphabet (plastic letters children can arrange to spell words) before learning to write with a pencil (Seldin, 2006). One Montessori "ages and stages" chart, which defines what an average child can do at a certain age, will suggest that children are ready to write with a pencil when they are five or six years old (Britton, 1992). Children who learn to write before their hand muscles are ready often develop bad writing habits that take years of effort to break or have messy writing that is hard to read. There is no real benefit to making children write before they are ready. In fact, pushing children to write at an early age to the point where it tires out the child may lead to them disliking writing. I once had a student who was made to write the same words over and over again in an English immersion kindergarten. She came to my school at the age of six and was so traumatized by this experience that she refused to touch a pencil for half a year. Years later, she was still reluctant to write.

Waiting until children are developmentally ready to write doesn't mean that they cannot learn phonics or letter recognition. Very young children can learn letter shapes in many ways, such as playing with alphabet blocks or using their bodies or hands to make the letters (e.g. students can stand with their left arm straight up and their right arm and right leg at a 45-degree angle to make the letter "K"). Many Montessori kindergartens use sandpaper letters, so students can learn the letter shapes in a multi-sensory way by tracing the letters with their fingers. They can also color in bubble letters with crayons on a worksheet. Parents seem to be satisfied with these alternatives to writing, especially when reasons behind doing so are explained.

Another issue that has come up is left-handedness. Japanese traditionally hold a negative view of writing with the left hand because calligraphy is done using a brush (Hatta & Kawakami, 1995; Shimizu & Endo, 1983). While most people these days recognize that forcing a child who is left-handed to write with their right hand confuses the brain (Spock & Parker, 1998), this belief may still persist (Japan Today, 2017), at least among some of the parents I have come across. Twenty years ago, some parents expressed concern to the office staff that having a left-handed teacher like me would result in their children not learning how to write English letters properly. One parent went so far as to ask me to discourage her daughter from using her left hand to write. When I tried to explain that this confuses the brain, she became angry and accused me of not understanding Japanese culture because "all Japanese know" it is "impossible" to do calligraphy well with your left hand. After this interaction with the mother, I was asked by the office staff to abide by the parent's wishes. I refused to comply and told the office staff that I would drop the issue but would not force any child to write with their right hand. Later, I wrote about this experience in an internet group for eikaiwa school owners and was extensively criticized by one school owner, who felt it was wrong of me to go against the mother's wishes. Luckily, this has not been an issue I have had to deal with in recent years.

Children taking adult tests

> *"My son passed level 3 of the Eiken in kindergarten and now he's having trouble passing level pre-2."*

The *Eiken* test is one of the most widely used English tests in Japan (*Eiken* Foundation of Japan, 2019). It is a test designed for students of junior high school age and older and passing Level 1 or 2 can allow easier entry into a private junior or senior high school. The *Eiken* Junior test is a listening test designed for children, but as this only tests listening skills, many parents prefer their children to take what they see as the "real *Eiken*" instead. The Cambridge YLE test, a four skills test that is designed for children and popular around the world, is not very well known in Japan and there are few places available for students to take it.

As the results of the *Eiken* test are only valid for two years, there is no real practical reason for students under the age of ten to take it. Despite the fact that it is a test designed for teenagers and adults, thousands of young children take this test every year. In 2012, over 200,000 elementary school aged children took the exam. Of those, 2,410 were five-year-olds and 4,200 were six-year-olds (The Japan Times, 2013). News articles and stories about very young children passing the higher levels of the *Eiken* garner a lot of attention and admiration in mainstream Japanese society, such as one case where a teacher helped a six-year-old boy pass Level pre-1 and then later helped another six-year-old pass Level pre-2.

In the past, I often had students come to my school who were graduates of international English-immersion pre-schools. Many of the parents who send their children to these schools cannot speak English themselves and therefore cannot objectively judge how much English their child knows. As the schools were under pressure to reassure the parents that their children had developed their English skills, it seems it was common practice for those schools to have their kindergarten students take Level 3 of the *Eiken* test, simply because at that time it was the lowest level of the test with a speaking test. (Since 2017, Levels 4 and 5 of the *Eiken* test have an optional online speaking test [Shearon, 2017]). While taking these tests may have satisfied parental wishes, there were often lasting consequences. I met graduates of these immersion schools who could read and speak well, yet could not pass Level 3 because they were not mature enough to handle the pressures of taking a test designed for adults. These students who had failed the test at such a young age often concluded that they were not as good at English as they had imagined and lost confidence in their abilities.

The kindergarteners who passed the test, naturally wanted to take the next level. Unfortunately, once they began studying for Level 2 and up, they found they were not only being tested on their English skills, but also on their ability to give opinions and answer questions on adult topics, such as paternity leave and real estate values. One student told me how she was confused during the Level 2 speaking test because she did not have any idea what the testing examiner meant when he asked her a question about e-commerce. I have witnessed first-hand and heard stories about children losing their motivation when taking tests that are cognitively above them, regardless of their language skills. Their lack of success with passing the next level of the *Eiken* test led to them becoming unmotivated to continue studying English. On the other hand, young students who somehow managed to pass Level 2 often declared that they had achieved their ultimate goal (determining that Level pre-1 was beyond their reach) and were no longer motivated to study English because they felt there was nothing left to strive for. Most of these students were around the age of nine, the age when many students in Japan start thinking about beginning *juken*, studying for private junior/senior high entrance examinations, so they completely stopped studying English in order to concentrate on those exams. It was sad to see them quit studying, as I knew they would suffer language loss and probably never regain their high proficiency in English.

There are some eikaiwa schools that advertise on their websites the success they have had with their students passing the test. One such school advertises that students can begin preparing for the *Eiken* test at the age of two. This puts the eikaiwa school owners like me, who are aware of the potential harm in having children take tests designed for adults, in a difficult situation. School owners understand that they could attract more students if they accommodated parental requests and offered a curriculum that helped study for the tests. In the past few years, there have been very heated debates on Facebook teacher groups in Japan between school owners who support young children taking the *Eiken* and school owners who do not, despite there being no empirical evidence to support such beliefs. This continues to be a very controversial subject amongst school owners in Japan, as well as being difficult to educate the parents of students about.

Conclusion

When I was a child, I took ballet lessons from a well-respected ballet school in my town. The teacher had a huge poster in the lobby, entitled, "Why Can't I Go on my Toes?" It clearly illustrated and explained why young children's bodies were not ready for toe shoes and how pushing young children to do something, simply because it looks good and pleases the parents, can have lasting harm. As a school owner, I have thought about that poster often and remember how my ballet teacher occasionally lost students because the parents wanted to see their daughters dance on their toes.

Most of the developmentally inappropriate practices described in this paper stem from schools or teachers bowing to pressure from well-meaning parents who push their children to do things at too early an age because they feel it will give them a future advantage. Medina (2014) termed this "hyper-parenting" (p. 152), a practice that can hurt a child's intellectual development as well as being counterproductive. Katz (1997) has also stated "just because children can do something . . . does not mean that they *should* do it . . . Young children can be coerced into learning and engaging in many activities that may not necessarily be in their best interests in the long term … but that may seem acceptable, insignificant, or harmless in the short term" (p. 18). These children can lose their natural interest in learning and exploring, a phenomenon Katz (1997) described as "second grade wash-out" (p. 18).

Most debate on EFL teaching methods at the adult level focuses on what is most effective, which is appropriate because adults have completed their development cycle. However, teachers of children, and especially of very young children, have a greater responsibility because children are still growing and what they do can have a great positive or negative impact on their development. School owners and teachers of children who realize the negative long term effects of what may seem to be effective for teaching children English in the short term, should feel confident in implementing their school's developmentally appropriate practices and be supported by all in the eikaiwa field. Furthermore, by reading and sharing research with parents, these teachers will have an easier time convincing them of the value of developmentally appropriate classroom practices.

7. Emotional labour in the eikaiwa classroom

Amelia Yarwood

Imagine a manila folder spread out in front of you. The client's file, as prepared by the scheduling staff, is filled with bold, red font and highlighted sections. The requests are numerous. Don't talk about his mother, art, movies or his job. Don't point at him. Don't talk too long. Don't cut him off when he is talking. Be specific in your feedback. Finish the lesson on time so that he doesn't have to wait at the counter afterwards. At the bottom of the file, boxed in red are two warnings. Firstly, that this client had previously yelled at the front counter staff for being 'too slow', and secondly, he had abruptly left another instructor's lesson because he hadn't been satisfied. The scheduling staff tell you that only certain instructors are given his lessons to teach.

A large part of an eikaiwa instructor's job is negotiating between the demands and desires of their varied clientele, their role as an employee at an English conversational school, and their own emotional states. Using my own experiences as a former eikaiwa instructor, and those of three other former employees who consented to be interviewed, this chapter will focus on the affective aspects of working in the eikaiwa industry. While many men and women are currently employed as conversation instructors, the individuals included in this chapter are all female. A single male was interviewed, however, time constraints limited his inclusion. Each of the individuals who participated in the semi-structured interviews were known to me either through work or post-graduate study and were chosen based on their willingness to share their experiences. Information about the purpose of the research was shared prior to each interview and everyone was asked to select a preferred pseudonym. The perspectives and experiences in this chapter belong to:

> **Emma** is a Taiwanese-born Canadian who had been teaching at smaller eikaiwa schools for about three years.
> **Julia** is Ukrainian. She worked for a large, well-known company within the eikaiwa industry for three years.
> **Sofía** hails from Columbia and worked for two years as both

a Spanish and English conversation instructor.

As with any form of work that necessitates close contact with people, language teaching can result in a gamut of emotions being experienced. However, the power imbalances between the instructors, their clients and company expectations make the emotional side of working at an eikaiwa worthy of discussion.

Provision of a service

The teaching of English is a global business. In Japan, the attitude towards learning English is best illustrated by the terminology used in government policies whereby English has been described as *saiteigen no dogu* and *mottomo kihonteki na noryoku*: the "minimum tool" and the "most basic skills" (Kawai, 2007, p.44). This language as used in official MEXT documents (2002) appeared to have a tendency to neutralise the interpersonal aspect of the language and revealed a focus that was less about connecting people through language, but rather how English could contribute to Japan's economic success in an age of globalisation (Hashimoto, 2009). Government documents in 2012 (Cabinet Office, 2012, as cited in Yoshida, 2013) emphasised the need to cultivate human resources for global development. In doing so, official documents placed a focus on English as a tool for international communication with explicit reference to the development of "linguistic skills for bilateral negotiations" and "communication skills for business conversations and paperworks" (Cabinet Office, 2012, p. 8 as cited in Yoshida, 2013). MEXT documents outlining the English Educational Reform Plan that was to take place between 2014 and 2018 also included references to an economic priority with upper secondary classes being expected to include "high-level linguistic activities (presentations, debates, negotiations)" (MEXT, 2014). While government educational priorities may change, this attitude as presented by the government during the time many of our clients were educated, may account for the volume of clients who attend conversation schools in the hope of improving their English for career promotions, overseas business trips and interacting with foreign customers or clients. Although communication-focused, it is perhaps unsurprising that eikaiwa market their instructors in rather superficial terms. When portrayed, the eikaiwa instructor is frequently marketed in terms of their nativeness and whiteness (Bailey, 2006; Kubota, 2011a), which plays into the fantasy prospective learners have of a potential future in which their eikaiwa instructor will help them gain the social capital associated with being competent in using English (generally in a professional context) (Bailey, 2006). In reality, this is not always the case with many instructors having little to no background in teaching English as a second language, or having received limited training with the company's curriculum (Bossaer, 2003; Taylor, 2017).

> ...the students are being fooled by the company because the majority of the 'professionals' that the company employs have no education, no training, no idea what the language is like, have no idea how the language should be taught, have no idea about intercultural communication, conflict resolution or anything like this, but they are being sold to the students as someone who does have all those things and who is qualified in all of those things. (Julia)

> People [Instructors] who don't have any experiences or background whatsoever [in language education], who's not so interested in teaching, I feel that for them, they would be happy to just sit in silence for an hour. Or even just only talk themselves and have the students listen. I do see that pattern sometimes when the teacher just keeps on talking and the students says just one word answers here and there, which is not very professional. (Emma)

All of the women interviewed felt that hiring trends within their companies reflected this aspect of superficial marketing. The criteria for eikaiwa instructors appeared to be heavily focused on their "nativeness" and less on their qualifications.

> ...some eikaiwa really care about your accent...I remember one eikaiwa, and the person that I knew, he had an interview. He's Latin-American and they tell them that they are looking for somebody who talks standard Spanish and they meant Spanish from Spain which was quite rude to say to a Latin-American. It's like saying, I'm looking for a standard English other than British. They really care about your *mitame* (appearance). Yeah, it was quite superficial, let's say that. (Sofia)

> I feel like that the expectations, to be honest, as long as you are a native speaker you can get the job fairly easily. (Emma)

Sofia, who was hired as a Spanish and English instructor, recalled feeling a sense of disappointment from some of her clients when they learned that she was a non-native English speaker despite her qualifications.

> I think many students were quite disappointed when I was their English teacher. They were, "Where are you from?" I was like, "I`m from Columbia", and they were like "Whaaat?"

Despite experiencing reactions such as these, Sofia did mention that there were many clients who genuinely wanted to connect with other speakers of the language they were learning and who didn't care about accent but rather what instructors could teach them.

Demand for English language skills may account for the sheer number of untrained instructors working in eikaiwa around Japan but terminology may play a part in the continuation of this trend. The term "eikaiwa" translates to "English conversation", suggesting that the learning that takes place may be informal rather than formal, incidental rather than systematic. If the learning is not intended to be formal nor systematic, then trained individuals by extension are not required. Regardless of the semantics, eikaiwa are first and foremost businesses with a responsibility to their bottom line, and trained educators pose a risk to profit since they require higher salaries. The provision of a solely conversational service would, however, not be as profitable – there are countless apps and social communities who can fulfil the general conversational needs of clients.

Issues of power

Language teaching has thus been amalgamated into the eikaiwa business model and this is where the expectations between companies, clients and instructors begin to get murky. In an eikaiwa classroom or lesson interaction, one would assume that the clients, as new or continuing language learners, would prioritise their individual learning. However, in Julia's case, the offering of Business English lessons for company groups resulted in unusual interactions.

> ...sometimes there is a very strange power dynamic when you have a manager and somebody who is not a manager...You ask a question to everyone. For example, "Oh, so what do you guys think about spending your holiday in Japan instead of going abroad?" Nobody answers until the manager answers. And then everybody basically repeats what the manager said in different words. That's a weird dynamic.

In a traditional lesson, Julia, as the instructor, would have the power to bring to light this unusual interaction and encourage each participant to speak in accordance to their own thoughts and feelings. On the other hand, as a service provider, she was bound by the desires of the client. Therefore, to point out the obstacle this hierarchy presented in a language lesson may have gone against cultural norms and resulted in complaints being made against her. In other cases, such as Sofia's, frustration was experienced when clients misunderstood the purpose of lessons. One example she gave related to clients using coupons for three free-trial lessons believing that the translation of documents equated to studying and learning the language. Initially, Sofia would assist with translations out of a desire to help her clientele, but after repeat experiences with clients using the free-trial coupons, she began to feel that her prospective clients were taking advantage of her accessibility.

> So there are three *tameshi* (trial lessons) so maybe in the first one [they'll want translations] and then they're going to follow the class but if in the second lesson they continue with their crappy translation, I will say like, "I'm sorry. This is not my job."...But sometimes they were like, "oh no no, I don't want to do that." So it was frustrating because they were misunderstanding my job. I'm a teacher not a translator.

Issues in quality control

In an industry that is built on the premise of communicative learning, the quality of the interactions between the client and the instructor is integral to the success of business. Perhaps to ensure that interactions flow, many eikaiwa companies provide their own pre-prepared materials and textbooks. This enables instructors regardless of their experience to engage with the clients. However, as individuals with backgrounds in education, each of the participants expressed low job satisfaction within this kind of work environment.

> Cause it's eikaiwa it's incredibly boring. Cause you do, sometimes you teach the same lesson four, five times in a single day. Everything is always the same. You can not improvise, you can not do anything you like. (Julia)

> They [big eikaiwa companies] don't have a lot of high standards, you don't have a lot of freedom in the classroom. You're pretty much a human recorder so...there's not much fun if you actually have experience in teaching. (Emma)

It could be argued that provision of pre-prepared teaching materials is no different to textbooks used in high school classrooms, however a key difference is found in the freedom instructors have in modifying the presentation of these materials. Companies who produce their own materials or develop their own system of teaching may market themselves as more "professional," but due to this structured approach they also offer the least amount of freedom for instructors.

> We are not teachers, we are the vessels for the method that the company, you know, utilised as the main method for teaching. They expected you to follow the method, to be the vessel for the method, that's kinda I feel the company expectations. (Julia)

However, in other companies, instructors and clients appear to be able to negotiate the content that is covered in a lesson. This freedom may extend from the "conversational" perspective companies embody, meaning that their approach is less geared towards linguistic proficiency in a language but rather the enjoyable qualities of conversation.

Issues with selling conversation

The sale of "conversation," however, problematises the dynamic between the instructor and the client. Conversations are conventionally an exchange between two or more individuals during which the balance of power is shared. The speaker will control the conversation but only until the listener trades places. In an industry that sells conversation, it is generally the client who is able to dictate the terms of the conversation, and the company who endorses this power.

> If the client is happy, they are happy. If the client's not happy, they're not happy. So they want people that the client will like. So they don't need a strict teacher. They need someone who is flexible and who can talk to lots of different types of people. Different personalities who can get along with them so they don't get complaints from the clients and then repeats from the clients. (Emma)

Complaints from clients endanger the profits and reputation of the company. As a result, instructors are expected to not only provide instruction but also engaging conversation based on the clients' own interests. This can be emotionally draining for instructors when clients' needs become very specific or contrary to their own. One such example comes from Julia, who felt that as an instructor, her role was to provide guidance. However, not all her clients felt the same.

> Some students would say, "Please don't correct my mistakes." And they would flood you with this torrent of, I am sorry to say this, garbage language that doesn't make any sense, has no grammar. That is all over the place and that just makes your ears wither, and you're not supposed to correct them.

In my own case, there were clients who while expressing their preferences or opinions, would touch on subjects that made myself and my colleagues uncomfortable. In particular, one client expressed frequently and in a vehement manner his hatred for the American naval officers stationed in Okinawa. Undoubtedly, there is historical cause for his views, however, many instructors felt intimidated by this client's tirades and, in some cases, were personally attacked due to their own connections with the American Navy. As a paying client who regularly booked lessons, however, the solution offered by the company was to pair the client with non-American instructors while suggesting that the instructors themselves do their best to steer any conversation away from potentially sensitive or offensive topics. As an employee, it often felt that the clients' desires were the priority of the organisation rather than the comfort or security of its employees. Sofia in her interview told a story about a male client who after complimenting her on her hair, reached out to touch the ends of her hair by her collarbone. Her "don't" was responded to with laughter and while she was able to end the lesson without further incident, the support she received from her supervisors was non-confrontational in nature and unsatisfactory in Sofia's opinion.

> ...it bothers me that they didn't say anything to him. They just said, I mean I didn't want to see him ever so instead of telling him like "Hey, it's not okay to do that"...my boss, she was more like, "it is not that bad"...they didn't say anything. Like, from now your teacher will be another person and that's it.

In a similar vein, Julia shared her thoughts on company expectations in regard to more difficult clients.

> If the customer is crazy, and we had crazy people, you're supposed to be equipped to deal with their craziness and not let anything slip, you know, slip in terms of you panicking or being intimidated. You were supposed to cater to, you were not supposed to be a teacher.

The language Julia uses in her statement highlights the emotional strain of having to "cater to" the behaviours as exhibited by her clients. As shown in the above anecdotes, Julia, like Sofia and myself, was forced into situations where the 'professional' facade was expected to be maintained for the client's peace of mind. Uncomfortable conversation topics can be mitigated by following set materials that avoid sensitive subjects, but when clients are sold conversation-based classes, and are given the freedom to pursue "free conversation" or conversation that does not have an educational purpose in mind, then it can place instructors in potentially disturbing circumstances. This potential is exacerbated by the common one-on-one lesson format and company policies that do not appear to hold clients accountable for their behaviour, simply on the basis that they are a paying customer.

Provision of emotional support

Teaching is a profession which carries with it an "ethic of care" (Gilligan, 1982; Noddings, 1984), meaning that educators are expected to be aware of the emotions their students are experiencing, and act in accordance to encourage and motivate. Eikaiwa organisations as companies that advertise the development of language skills are not exempt from this "ethic of care" principle, meaning that eikaiwa instructors are expected to provide emotional support to their clients. When talking to Emma, Julia and Sofia, two distinct roles arose; that of the silent psychologist and motivational coach.

The silent psychologist

Humans by their very nature are said to make sense of their world through stories. The majority of conversations are narratives we tell about ourselves and our place in the world and so it may be unsurprising that some clients use conversation schools as an opportunity to tell their own stories.

> ..what I realised is that a lot of them are there as their hobby or their company told them to. They're not as motivated ...a lot of them are tired from work and just want someone to listen to their problems sometimes. (Emma)

Japan is well known as a society that tries its best to avoid conflict. Giving air to one's grievances, frustrations and concerns while cathartic, are viewed as not being conducive to maintaining a positive social image (Ohbuchi & Atsumi, 2010). For this reason, many clients may perceive their eikaiwa instructor as a loophole to this social dilemma. As a foreigner, the instructor is not bound by the cultural norms of Japanese society and as a representative of the more "open and liberal" West, the instructor may also be considered a safe option for expressing one's inner thoughts. For example, I recall one client who made repeat requests for lessons with a particular male instructor. While working in the booth next door, I overheard some of the conversation that was taking place, or rather the saga. When the lesson had ended and we were safely cloistered in an office, I asked the instructor if his client had always disclosed such intimate details of her rocky relationships to him. He confessed that it was the only type of conversation his client had ever been interested in and that he felt his role was simply to be a sympathetic ear.

In both Emma's and my examples, the notion of "listening" arises. Since the relationship is one in which the client has paid money for conversation, the power in this dynamic lies with the client. As Emma states,

> Well, as their instructor I am there to...I can't really say anything back to them to make them upset. So all I can do is listen to them and be, aw that's too bad and give them new words to describe how tired they are.

As mentioned earlier, the majority of eikaiwa instructors are not trained educators. Likewise, they are not trained in methods of dealing with emotionally unstable or frustrated individuals. Nor should they be. Unfortunately, the situation in Japan sees mental illness, depression and other negative emotions as something that should be hidden resulting in few individuals seeking professional help (Griffiths, 2006; Naganuma et al., 2006). The culture surrounding mental health in Japan means that eikaiwa instructors sometimes feel that they are being used as outlets, or as silent psychologists since even if a client seeks advice, instructors are untrained and unwilling to provide more than sympathy or linguistic help.

The motivational coach

For the interviewees and I who had education backgrounds, the role of a motivational coach is a familiar one since it is a role teachers often play in the classroom to elicit greater thinking or action in their students.

> I remember one student who knows, he was really good at grammar, vocabulary, better than me, well grammar rules, but he didn't talk about anything with me, and I was like, "No. You can't do that in real life so…" So it was more like motivating them. It was more like a coach. So that's how I saw myself. (Sofia)

A teacher who acts as a coach takes on a more interactive approach towards their students' motivation by guiding students through risk-free challenges, listening to them and simulating realistic learning activities (Stix & Hrbek, 2006). Emotions experienced in this role were generally positive. Encouraging an individual to reach higher is a rewarding action that is active and relatively immediate in nature. It bears little resemblance to the emotions at play while fulfilling the passive role of the silent psychologist. Unlike a coach who tends to work with those who have a passion for self-improvement, eikaiwa instructors are obliged to coach those who may not always be looking to improve. The clearest example of this can be found in anecdotes about salarymen who are forced to attend lessons because they have been paid for by their company. When I asked Emma about her negative experiences, she responded with the following comment:

> Negative experiences, I guess would be the students who are forced to be there. Who don't want to try and no matter how hard you try to get them to speak as much as possible in the one hour, they only do one word answers. They don't really elaborate...I think that's the most off-putting.

When discussing the back-to-back weekend lessons she had to teach, Julia stated that the mental toll of having to motivate and coax individuals who she was not able to connect well with manifested as exhaustion.

> If it doesn't click in that first lesson then you are destined to suffer for another 90 minutes. And it's just, it's just so draining. Sometimes when you go home, after the lesson on the weekend your body feels physically tired. You don't want to go anywhere. You feel so exhausted.

Each of these roles, the silent psychologist and the motivational coach, require instructors to act in a manner that will encourage and support their clients. During lessons where instructors feel bound by their lack of training, uncomfortable or otherwise unable to connect on a genuine level with their client, they are required by the expectations of the organisation to regulate their emotions for the sake of the client. Such regulation of emotions on an ongoing basis leads to burnout and reduced job satisfaction. To cope with the emotional fatigue experienced during burnout, instructors may diminish their responsibility to the client by objectifying or depersonalising them (Grandey, 2000). This coping mechanism was highlighted by Julia who made the following comment.

> Some people who have been with that company for a very long time, they just gave up on it. They knew all the lessons...And ah, they prided themselves on not preparing at all. "Oh, I don't care about this anymore, so I'm just going to come in and do whatever and er, wing it."

Final comments

The eikaiwa industry offers their clients much that their instructors are not often trained to provide. The vagueness of what constitutes "conversation" forces instructors to become multi-talented conversationalists, educators, psychologists and translators. These factors and the privileges organisations provide their clients mean that burnout and low job satisfaction are common among eikaiwa instructors. The stories shared by former eikaiwa instructors only emphasise that more needs to be done to improve the imbalances that exist and subsequently improve the quality of instructors' well-being while working in Japan's conversation schools.

8. Exploring the differences between eikaiwa and business English

Christopher Maschio

I was initially employed for 10 years by a small, foreign-owned corporate training company that specialised in business-to-business customised training programs for students working in large Japanese and global companies. During these years, my experience in oral communication assessment, program development, materials design and teaching was limited to the business English (BE) context, which is "an approach to language teaching, course design and material development in which all decisions as to context and methods are based on the learners' reasons for learning" (Hutchinson & Waters, 1987, cited in Chibi, 2018, p. 197). Then, in 2013, the company was fully integrated into a global English language school. In the years following integration, I learned about the inner workings of a global language school, or eikaiwa, through my involvement in their material design, program development, and initial teacher training program. All the while, I continued to service the corporate clients taking BE courses from my former employer, which had been renamed and turned into a department of the English language school. In this chapter, I will explore the similarities and differences between the two contexts regarding employee recruitment, methods and approaches to classroom instruction, and assessment. I will also look at how working in the two different contexts impacted my identity as a teacher and provide some recommendations that could enhance the quality of education that large eikaiwa schools provide in Japan.

Employee recruitment

Before the 2013 integration of my employer, a foreign-owned corporate training company, into a global language school, I held the belief that large chain eikaiwa schools in Japan generally only recruited native-speaking English teachers from inner-circle countries where English was spoken as a first language. I was, however, pleasantly surprised following integration with the progressive recruitment policies of my new employer to fill teaching and specialist positions, such as content developers or programs designers. This is because close to half of the recruits that fit the school's "native fluency" criteria for employment (i.e. most of their education had been in English speaking institutions) were from non-native English speaking countries. In fact, diversity was encouraged throughout all departments of the school. For example, a division in the eikaiwa context tasked with teaching low proficiency students and TOEIC preparation courses only employed teachers who were proficient in both Japanese and English, with a preference for teachers whose L1 was Japanese. The school in the eikaiwa context also demonstrated an inclusive hiring policy when it came to gender diversity, employing only a slightly higher proportion of male teachers to female teachers.

From an educational point of view, I feel that the school believed that this diversity allowed students to become familiar with various accents and cultural differences. As a result, students would be better prepared to communicate with a wider variety of people outside of the classroom. I also presume that teacher diversity was a point of differentiation from its competitors that may not have been as progressive with their teacher recruitment. I think, however, the advantages of a diverse pool of teachers ran much deeper. From what I observed, when providing training to and with nonnative English-speaking teachers, regardless of their teaching qualifications and experience, they were generally compassionate and took a genuine interest in teaching and the challenges faced by their students. This empathy, I presume, was brought about by them being a learner of the language at one point in their life and therefore understanding the challenges their students face.

Unfortunately, in terms of recruitment for the BE side of the operations, teacher ethnicity and gender diversity weren't as broad as in the eikaiwa context. From what I observed, this disparity, however, was not because of a policy promoting the belief that native-speaker teachers represent a "Western culture" (Holliday, 2005 cited in Holliday, 2006, p. 385) or because of a preference for male teachers over female teachers. In fact, the BE context welcomed applications from potential female employees in an attempt to satisfy the demands placed on it from its corporate clients wanting greater diversity among its teachers. Instead, the disparity was caused by a lack of female applicants possessing experience in corporate work and English language teaching. At my school, this underrepresentation of female teachers in the BE context was a phenomenon I witnessed throughout my entire time in the BE field, with females only occupying 5 to 10 % of all teaching positions.

Methods and approaches to material development and classroom instruction

The methods and approaches to material development and classroom instruction varied greatly between the eikaiwa and BE contexts. The eikaiwa context had a set teaching approach and method, which according to its sales documents, had "evolved in line with the latest research and technology" and that students "learn grammar as a means of communication." Additionally, when developing materials for this context, I was required to follow a 40-minute lesson cycle that included 6 key lesson stages and write a teaching script that outlined how each lesson should be taught. In contrast, the approach in the BE context was more flexible with regards to the development of materials and in-class instruction. Materials did not need to be developed based on a particular lesson cycle or style of instruction. Moreover, I had the freedom to prepare my own lessons plans and make my own teaching decisions.

In the eikaiwa context, I was given very little room to diverge from the use of a standard Present, Practice and Production teaching approach and curriculum was organised according to something akin to what Ellis & Shintani (2014) have described as a "contemporary grammatical syllabus where grammar is not just an inventory of forms but acknowledges the form-meaning mapping that lies at the heart of grammar" (p. 55). The eikaiwa context also prided itself on its adherence to five key principles:

1) Exclusive use of the language
2) Speaking and listening supported by reading and writing
3) Grammar as a means of communication
4) Maximum learner participation
5) Goal orientated, lively instruction based on the learner's needs and interests

Although it could be disputed that reading and writing were used to support speaking and listening, as I rarely saw examples of in-house materials that contained reading and writing activities, the school strictly followed the other four principles. I believe that this tightly controlled structure was conducive to the deployment of logically structured lessons. Moreover, it also helped ensure consistency from lesson to lesson and was a means by which the school regulated lesson quality as many of the teachers had little, if any teaching experience. In addition to the in-class benefits "the method" provided, I also felt that it was an important marketing tool that helped drive sales as it provided a kind of insurance of quality to potential students.

Regardless of the advantages "the method" brought to the company, I grew more and more frustrated with it and the PPP approach the longer I was involved in this context. From a curriculum development perspective, writing materials based on a specific lesson cycle, one or two grammar points, and the need to include specific activities in each section of the lesson from a master set of prescribed lesson activities made lessons overly predictable and reduced student engagement in the learning process. The frustration I felt also extended to the teachers. Due to the sheer weight of their workload - with many teaching up 10, 45-minute lessons per day and little room to inject personal creativity into lessons, a lack of teacher motivation was a major issue. Nevertheless, I and many other employees did what was expected of us, as failure to do so would result in a poor evaluation from management. As one former college explained, teachers generally didn't buy into the methodology used at the school, however, they were obliged to use it for "fear of repercussions."

In the BE context, there was no prescribed teaching approach I was required to follow. However, the approach I adopted in this context resembled something similar to Task-Based Language Teaching (TBLT). Defined by Ellis (2009) as "the principle that language learning will progress most successfully if teaching aims simply to create contexts in which the learner's natural language learning capacity can be nurtured rather than making a systematic attempt to teach the language bit by bit" (p. 222), TBLT was a good fit for BE. This was because it provided a framework I could use that allowed me to focus on the accomplishments of specific tasks relevant to the students' needs in their workplace rather than breaking a course syllabus into individual grammar points. Moreover, I felt that many students were discontent with conventional approaches to teaching that prioritised grammatical accuracy and explicit language instruction over lessons that were meaning or task-focused in which attention to linguistic forms came via brief corrective feedback.

Although the freedom I had in the BE context helped to counterbalance the growing resentment I had towards the constraints of eikaiwa, the luxury to essentially do what I wanted as far as material design and in-class instruction was concerned occasionally made it difficult to ensure consistency between classes without resorting to the use of a teaching script, as was required in the eikaiwa context. I especially found this to be the case when developing programs and materials for other teachers to use. To overcome the problem of trying to ensure a certain level of quality without lessons being overly prescriptive, I had what were known as "pre-course meetings" with teachers to explain the needs of the student and how I thought the materials I developed and/or the published textbook I had selected could be best used to achieve the learning objectives of a particular course of study. I also encouraged teachers to explain how they could envisage the course unfolding and to think about how tasks and/or activities could be modified to ensure they meet the specific needs of their students. Over time, I have also come to appreciate different teaching approaches to my own. Moreover, I also recognise that teaching the student in front of me rather than worrying about adherence to a specific teaching style or approach is of utmost importance in the language classroom.

Despite the differences between eikaiwa and BE, one area in which I felt both contexts were similar was the lack of attention given to self-directed learning (SDL). Although attempts were made to encourage self-study through the development of online, in-house homework exercises in the eikaiwa context, no attention was given to the teaching of language learning strategies or pointing students in the direction of resources they could use outside of the classroom to learn independently and take control of their learning (Benson, 2011). This apparent lack of interest from both teaching contexts in SDL could be attributed to several factors, namely a limited understanding of the benefits of SDL by those employed at the eikaiwa in which I worked and a need to ensure students kept enrolling in programs.

Before starting my MA TESOL degree in 2016, I certainly didn't understand the potential benefits SDL could have and was a teacher that simply assigned homework from the coursebook. However, while undertaking my studies and in the time following their completion, I have come to understand that students who are guided to learn how to study by themselves are generally more proactive learners. A more cynical view that may explain the lack of attention given to SDL in my context, however, could be that the language school was essentially a big business that has financial commitments to its shareholders. As such, it wasn't in their financial interests to create an environment that promoted student control and independent learning outside of the classroom. When I quizzed the director of the department responsible for the development of materials in both the eikaiwa and BE teaching contexts about the possibility of expanding the school's resources to encourage learner autonomy and self-directed learning, he was rather dismissive of the idea, believing that students may purchase fewer lessons if they "can do it themselves."

Assessment

Both the eikaiwa and BE contexts had devised in-house assessments to test oral proficiency and listening comprehension. On the surface, the tests appeared similar. They were both administered over 15 to 20 minutes before the start of a course and at its completion. Moreover, neither context tested students' writing. It could be argued, however, that the similarities between the two approaches to assessment ended there.

Assessment in the BE context was high stakes, as the results affected promotion opportunities, were used to screen candidates before hiring, and in some cases the outcome of the assessment determined if a student would have the language proficiency to be posted on an overseas assignment. Because of this, all proficiency interviews were recorded and independently double rated by trained, in-house assessors. The oral proficiency interview in the BE context was divided into three equally weighted areas and attempted to determine the communicative competence of client company employees through the assessment of the following areas:

- Language proficiency, which focused on vocabulary, grammar, pronunciation, flow of speech and listening comprehension;
- Delivery, which focused on eye contact, confidence in manner (the apparent degree of comfort or nervousness when conveying information) and;
- Communication of information, which assessed the use of supporting evidence, the degree to which ideas were coherent and logically ordered, and the willingness to share information.

Based on the outcome of this assessment, my colleagues and I in the curriculum department were able to assign level-appropriate materials and provided the students, and perhaps more importantly, the human resources department that was footing their training program fee, with a benchmark score to compare with their post-course score. In terms of validity, I felt the assessment was valid because it measured communicative proficiency via oral output, the linguistic feature it aimed to assess. On the other hand, my main criticism of this type of assessment in the BE context was that it didn't accurately assess what had taken place in class. This was because the courses that I generally taught and designed were task-based and focused on specific skills such as meeting participation, making presentations, and participating in negotiations, as per the request of most client companies prior to commencement of a course. The test, however, was an interview that touched on business-related and general topics but failed to accurately assess the achievements students had made on specific work-related tasks they had studied in the program. I feel that task-based assessment focusing on what took place in the class would be more appropriate, as it provides information about learners' abilities to use language in specific situations and better connects what a student does during the test and what they are required to do outside of a classroom. Moreover, it assesses what a student can do in more functional terms.

In contrast to the high-stakes nature of assessment in the BE context, assessment in eikaiwa was decidedly more low-stakes. In this oral proficiency assessment commonly known as a "level check", students were asked a series of questions and assigned a level based on their use of grammar, word choice, and pronunciation. The tests were not recorded and, as a result, they were not double rated. Teachers I spoke with felt that rather than the interviews being assessed based on the rubric the school had made, a lot of "intuition" went into the assessment. Similar opinions about the lack of reliability and the inability of the assessment to produce consistent results were even shared by senior management. In addition to these shortcomings, students didn't receive the results of their level check. Instead, they were almost always simply assigned a new level and offered a new course of study that would necessitate the purchase of more in-house developed textbooks. Although the school got away with these rather loose standards towards assessment, I felt that it was a disservice to the students who undertook the level check. Not only did it potentially provide some students with an inaccurate account of their language skills, but it was also almost exploitative in the sense that incorrect information was provided to students in an attempt to generate profit through the sale of in-house produced textbooks and additional courses.

Conclusion

After adjusting to the differences working for a global English language school presented and juggling material development and program design responsibilities in the eikaiwa and BE contexts, I decided to resign from my position six years after integration. Although my decision was difficult because of the strong relationships I had formed working with many dedicated colleagues and the stability of employment with a large company provided, in the end, I felt it was the right one. This is because since I started my MA TESOL program three years earlier, I had become increasingly disillusioned with the approaches to language learning and testing the eikaiwa supported. Moreover, I grew tired of working for a large company where I felt that I couldn't make a great deal of change. In spite of these negative feelings, my time in eikaiwa did positively impact on my identity as a teacher in a variety of ways. Firstly, exposure to different approaches to teaching and material development allowed me to critically evaluate what I observed and incorporate the most positive aspects in my teaching practice. Moreover, working in a sleek teaching context, driven by profit that made teachers accountable for every minute of lesson time taught me about the importance of efficiency. Lastly, my time spent in eikaiwa gave me an insight into the influence of marketing, and the necessity for a large company operating in this space to not only provide education but market their service in a way that is novel and sets it apart from its competitors if they are to continue to attract new students. Although my observations, thoughts, and conclusions working for a large eikaiwa school in Japan cannot be generalised, I hope that they resonate with teachers and material developers employed in a similar context.

9. "Don't repeat after me!": The transformation of an eikaiwa

Ruth Iida

Make your way up the clanging metal staircase of a grey building in the countryside of Hadano City, Japan and you'll see a startlingly colorful sign reading *Rainbow Phonics English School.* That's my workplace: an after-school study space for primary and secondary school children and a morning conversation café for 25 adults. On the weekends, it's used by high school and college students, who come to speak, sing, and make sense of their lives while using their second language. Of the school's current 115 students enrolled, only four receive private lessons; the remainder of the students participate in small group lessons, often spending six or more years together with the same classmates.

The school's beginning

Rainbow Phonics was originally a room in the family home shared by my Japanese husband and myself, my parents-in-law, and my two children. When I began teaching in 1999, I was the only blue-eyed blonde-haired woman in the neighborhood. I had no trouble attracting students simply on those credentials and although my prices were cheap, I made a tidy profit every year. My teaching qualifications consisted of a 6 week TESOL course in the U.S. and my curriculum and materials were developed on the fly. In spite of this, there were no enquiries about my resume or complaints about my handmade alphabet worksheets.

Neighborhood children formed the base of my primary level classes. Their mothers became my adult students and eventually my friends. Having a comfortable command of Japanese, I did not hesitate to use my students' first language to put my adult learners at ease and prevent awkward silences. I also used it to keep children in line, to charm them into good behavior, and to make classroom management easier for myself. All families involved seemed happy with that arrangement and it was easier for me to use Japanese than adapting my own speech to be more comprehensible to a non-native speaker. To be honest, I did not expect students to understand my unscripted English outside of the classroom.

As enrolment continued to increase, I moved to the grey concrete building downtown to preserve my family's privacy. My adult students became my staff, taking on reception duties, financial management, and the school's physical upkeep. Those who were confident in their English skills acted as class assistants as well. And so, with a minimum of fuss and fanfare, I became a school owner and manager as well as head teacher. Rainbow Phonics continued to thrive for the next ten years with no advertising apart from word of mouth. According to in-house surveys filled out by the parents of our young learners, they valued our school not only for academic reasons, but because of the low-stress learning environment, the warm and welcoming staff members, the elaborate seasonal parties, the cheap lesson fees, and the fact that their children developed positive attitudes toward language learning. Since the changes implemented in my young learner classes will be the focus of this chapter, I will not touch on adult classes. Instead, I will briefly describe a 50-minute elementary age learner's lesson in the early Rainbow Phonics days.

Rainbow Phonics as it was: A typical day

Most students arrived at the school well before their lesson time in order to enjoy a snack served in the reception area. They enjoyed playing with my own children's cast-off toys or chatting with the assistant teacher and receptionist in Japanese until class time began. Once students entered the actual classroom, good manners were expected and strictly enforced. Each child sat on a flat Japanese cushion in a perfectly arranged circle during speaking and singing time; veering off those cushions, rolling over backwards, or sitting in a disorderly fashion were not tolerated. We stood up and moved around for especially lively songs, but every child knew to return to their own cushion at the end. I dictated the rules like a friendly-but-firm mother and the rules were nearly always respected. I was confident and in control, always on guard against potential troublemaking, accidental injury, imminent nosebleeds or asthma attacks, misunderstandings, hurt feelings, or infectious cases of bad attitude. After circle time, students moved to the table area for phonics and writing time. Their seats were determined by me. After each child had completed the day's worksheet, they were allowed to choose a sticker before heading home. The routine rarely varied. I was at the center of a well-organized and happy universe.

What content did I teach to these primary age learners? In a nutshell, I taught any words or phrases that seemed appropriate for young EFL learners to remember, in the order of what seemed simplest to me. I presented the target English vocabulary in Japanese, keeping up a lively pace and encouraging lots of repetition. Especially in the lower primary years, my syllabus was song based, with themes built around songs I remembered from my own childhood or from my own children's early preschool years in the U.S. Along with the songs, I taught sets of things: colors, numbers, animals, food, toys, weather, days of the week, months, clothing, and other standard themes for young learners.

In those ten years, the majority of my students developed excellent listening skills, as measured by their near-perfect *Eiken* examination scores. Their pronunciation and intonation were clear and comprehensible to native speaker classroom visitors. Most of them became proficient readers. Some of them enjoyed writing and a very few enjoyed speaking enough to plunge into speech contests, ace their *Eiken* exam interviews, and enrol in study abroad programs. My staff told me our school was awesome, and since I had not visited other schools or engaged in any sort of professional development, there was no evidence to the contrary in my own mind.

The transition begins

In 2011, however, I finally became aware of other language teachers and English school owners. The Great East Japan quake, the tsunami, and the nuclear meltdown that devastated the Tohoku region of Japan shook me out of my complacency and compelled me to attend anti-nuclear demonstrations in Tokyo; it was there that I began meeting other English teachers and learning about local and global teaching and academic networks. Gradually, my passion extended from attending anti-nuclear demos to attending language teaching workshops and seminars. Eventually, in 2015, I enrolled in the TESOL graduate program at Temple University in Tokyo.

By temporarily closing Rainbow Phonics, I was able to finish my degree in a year and a half. It was rough. I had been out of school for twenty-eight years and was technologically challenged. On the other hand, having excellent compensational strategies and a genuine love of reading, writing, and studying that had been latent for years, I was able to enjoy and even savor my time in academia. Since most students in my program were hoping to land a stable teaching position at the university level, I was probably a bit of a curiosity to them; I simply hoped to go back to my original position and be a better teacher than I had been.

And I did go back to Rainbow Phonics. My last Temple class finished up in August 2016 and I returned to teaching in September that same year, armed with new insight into how learners learn and buoyed by energy and confidence. When drawing up the plans for my school's re-opening, the first hurdle I knew I had to clear was the challenge of sufficient and richer input. My students needed more time spent studying English on a weekly basis and better quality input during class time. Along with this, I was determined to push output and shift from a highly-controlled teacher-centered classroom to a more student-centered dialogic classroom. Lastly, I wanted to retain the trust and intimacy I had always had with students without using an excess of Japanese. In a nutshell, the five challenges I faced were sufficient input, better quality input, pushed output, achieving a dialogue with my students, and retaining intimacy while using more English.

Providing more input

The sobering realization of how much input my students needed was brought home to me in an article by Larson Hall where it was found that learners who had received minimal English input on a weekly basis from a young age (i.e. eikaiwa students) showed only "modest benefits" in phonology and morphosyntax and only after input substantially increased (Larson-Hall, 2006, p. 56). I wanted more than modest benefits for my students, yet I doubted that parents would be willing to increase English time by enrolling their children in classes twice a week. Instead, I chose to set longer class times, even for the youngest students. I also decreased vacation time to ensure more lessons per year.

In addition to this, I instigated a homework system, from age four on upwards, reasoning that homework was both input and practice time outside of the classroom. Using Nation's *Four Strands* (2007) as a touchstone, I scoured YouTube for the most enticing song, chant, and story videos to assign as homework, in the interest of providing meaning-focused input that children would want to engage with. Along with video watching, I prepared weekly reading assignments and written work and purchased enough books to start a small extensive reading borrowing library. As a result of promoting both homework and extensive reading vigorously to parents, the majority of families are now on board with the program: assigned reading gets done, worksheets are turned in, videos are watched, and students who do not do the out-of-class work usually fall behind and quit within a year.

The challenge of better input

Changing the quality of input during class time was actually the greater challenge, as it meant abandoning my own personal teaching style, which was heavily dependent on Japanese and sometimes even Japanized English expressions. Rod Ellis has written that ideally, the L2 should be "the medium as well as the object of instruction" (Ellis, 2005, p. 217) and after graduate school I knew I needed to move out of my comfort zone and begin teaching English in English. Giving instructions and explanations and making small talk in Japanese meant that my learners were actually getting much less than an hour a week's worth of input. This was no longer acceptable to me and I resolved to plunge into a more principled approach. Specifically, speaking, listening, and vocabulary-building activities (roughly 80% of younger learners' lesson time) would be conducted all in English, with ten to fifteen minutes of alphabet stories and writing instructions in Japanese. The older elementary classes would follow a similar pattern, with only grammar explanations and discussion of learning strategies in Japanese. I would make an effort to replace Japanese English phrases such as "level up" with more natural English expressions.

Although it took some time, I have become better at identifying my own descent into "Japanglish" and I've asked my assistants to check me as well. Moreover, after experimenting with my own word choices, I now feel more comfortable simplifying or elaborating my explanations in English, using gestures to enhance meaning and thinking on my feet as I speak: Will this explanation be salient to a six-year-old? Should I try phrasing it differently? Most importantly, having spent hours in graduate school poring over both computational and sociocultural models of language acquisition, I feel confident that learners are capable of comprehending not just the day's target words, but also instructions, praise and reprimands, error corrections, requests, and commands in English. In short, I have found that conducting a young learners class nearly entirely in English is absolutely doable for me.

Changing my medium of instruction to English has meant discarding many of the sentimental songs from my own childhood that needed explanations in Japanese. In fact, my repertoire of classroom songs has changed radically. My iPod playlist is now full of music created especially for language learning and easily available to parents through YouTube videos. Music is motivational but it is also input, and I no longer use singable songs that eat up time without reinforcing useful phrases or vocabulary. Also, because I now strive to show words in context, I have re-made most of my cards sets: the cat card now reads "a cat" and "sky" is labelled "the sky". Another card reads "on the hill". The process of refining classroom input is ongoing.

Pushing output

Along with more and richer input, I also knew that my students needed to be pushed to produce more language, especially unscripted language. From the beginning of my teaching days, I had been reluctant to push students who preferred to listen rather than contribute during class time. I did not have the patience to endure awkward silences nor the skills to circumvent them. Why disturb the status quo by forcing students to go against their natural inclinations? However, after reading Swain's analysis of French immersion studies done in Canada during the 1970's and 1980's (Swain, 1985), I knew that those arguments were no longer viable. Swain's analysis clearly showed that in spite of receiving rich input in a second language on a daily basis for seven years, non-native French speaking students had significantly lower scores than native speakers of the same age in both grammar and sociolinguistic aspects, as a result of not being pushed to produce output or negotiate for meaning. Swain's comprehensible output hypothesis (p. 249) proposed that communicative breakdowns and negative input push learners to try harder to convey their message. In essence, she claimed that "....one learns to speak by speaking" (p. 248). At the time of my school's re-opening, I did not yet have a strategy for pushing reluctant learners to speak, but I determined to at least look for opportunities.

Three years later, I've found that as I make a greater effort to *communicate* rather than *teach* in English, student output naturally follows, especially in the nursery and low elementary level classes. Surprisingly, it has not been necessary to endure a lot of awkward silence. Nation (2000, p. 8) has argued that course designers would do well to remember that "….words should occur in normal communication situations, not in contrived language-focused activities," and as I moved away from teaching sets of words, I saw students begin to use more language as they became more emotionally involved. For example, as I began pairing my "things in a house" cards with verb cards ("Turn on the lamp!" "Open the window!") and setting up situations that necessitated the use of those phrases, speaking time grew progressively livelier. Students began attempting to give advice and produce results rather than focusing on decontextualized language forms. As I fed students the phrases they needed to interact with me and with our bilingual staff, lessons became far more enjoyable than repeating the names of items and using them in games, especially when students began offering appropriate comments spontaneously. I'm pleased to report that these days I rarely use the phrase "Repeat after me!"

Encouraging students to experiment with language rather than produce the "right answer" has also led to more and better output. Hattie (2012) has written that, "Errors invite opportunities… they are exciting, because they indicate tension between what we now know and what we could know; they are signs of opportunities to learn and they are to be embraced," (p. 139-40). As I stopped focusing on learning words apart from context and began challenging my students to solve problems, give advice, and produce results, mistakes became part of the process, rather than an embarrassment to be avoided. Now there is often happy consternation when students' mistaken commands result in unexpected reactions ("I'm dirty, so I should go to bed?!") and I see children working together to repair mistakes rather than sinking into silence.

The challenge of dialoguing

Related to the challenge of pushing student output was the challenge of creating a more dialogic classroom. Hattie (2012) has rejected the common scenario of teachers as the owners of subject content and students as passive respondents to closed questions. "Many students learn to 'play the game' and thus are physically present, passively engaged, but psychologically absent," argued Hattie (p. 81). I wanted the opposite of that scenario, yet I had an uneasy feeling that moving away from teacher-centered presentations of language would mean outright chaos.

Swallowing my anxiety, I began by throwing out open-ended questions and comments designed to provoke responses. If social interaction is essentially the convergence of input and output (Ellis, 2005, p. 219), then I knew that to promote dialogue I needed to retire my role as drill master and pronunciation model and reinvent myself as an instigator of commentary. It was often a frustrating process. Shortly after reopening the school, for example, my students expected to be "taught." Dutifully repeating every question I asked them, the classroom soon became a mutually bewildering echo chamber. I learned to then ask the same question to my assistant, who would give an appropriate reply in English. That did the trick, and I began using my assistants to show appropriate patterns and responses rather than relying on them mainly for classroom management. The four-year-olds followed the assistant's example eagerly, beginning to personalize their own answers as they intuited meaning. Eventually, all the students caught on to the fact that lessons were set up as dialogues rather than drills and that they were expected to participate rather than memorize language. For some, it was a pleasant surprise: they had expected "lessons" but in fact got an unscripted yet well-organized playtime.

I had always taken pride in my ability to create and maintain order in the classroom; it was inevitable that changing my teaching style would lead to a modicum of chaos and unpredictability, but I found myself unexpectedly comfortable with that. A small amount of chaos, in fact, has been conducive to a more dialogic classroom approach. With no "raise your hand to speak" rule, students tend to respond spontaneously to questions that interest them without being called on. It can get noisy, but it's generally the good kind of noise: students enthusiastic about a game, a topic, or a new discovery. As far as seating, boundaries are no longer neatly marked by cushions, making it easier to physically interact for pair work and group work. Lastly, I no longer refer to myself as "teacher" in Japanese. Students now call me "Ruthie" rather than "Ruthie Sensei". I felt half naked at first, but was determined to present myself as a friend rather than an authoritarian figure. After all, it's easier for small children to disagree with and challenge a friend than a teacher and I want to be challenged and questioned. I still have the aura of a confident mother and thus far, chaos has not descended on Ruthie's classroom.

Snack time and the L1

Lastly, the challenge of preserving the intimacy I valued with students has been solved by a mid-lesson snack. Crackers and tea before class has been replaced by a five to seven-minute snack break between all-English speaking time and writing time. During this time, students are allowed to chat freely in Japanese about their school day, their friends, or any topic they want to share. I listen intently, adding a few words of encouragement or congratulations as appropriate, mentally fitting together the puzzle pieces of each child's personality. In all honesty, everyone including myself probably wishes that snack time was longer than seven minutes; I look forward to seeing my elementary age learners as high school and college students, when they have enough sophisticated vocabulary and grammar skills to freely discuss their daily lives in English.

In conclusion

Finally, I must also admit that my completion of the Temple graduate program itself was a huge boost of positivity for my school. As I mentioned before, most MS (Master of Science) students move "up" to become university instructors and very few eikaiwa schools retain classroom teachers with a graduate degree in education. When I re-opened Rainbow Phonics, many former students and new families attended my presentations on second language learning and most enrolled their children immediately. Slowly, my staff and I are working to change our reputation from a welcoming and easy-going school that demanded little commitment besides weekly attendance to a more meaning-focused, communicative study space that requires a greater time commitment and more active participation. Our enrolment numbers, retention rate, and comments from parents and students indicate that Japanese families in our area are open to this approach and are willing to invest both time and money for longer and more challenging language lessons. How effective the changes I have begun implementing remains to be seen. When my now-elementary age students reach college age, it's my hope that they will be able to use their interlanguage eagerly and fluently and to consider English as their second language rather than a subject they wrestled with in school. It's a good bet that I'll still be in Hadano by then, sipping coffee in the school with the colorful doors, ready for them to stop by anytime and tell me—in English—about their lives.

10. Eikaiwa vs. *juku*: The affordances and constraints of each context

Ewen MacDonald

Starting out in the private education market

As can be seen from official government data (METI, 2019b), eikaiwa and *juku* are both large and profitable multi-billion yen industries in the private education market in Japan. My foray into these teaching contexts began when I accepted a teaching position at a *juku* that was establishing a new English program. *Juku* are private cram schools that provide supplementary education to students for various subjects in order to prepare and support them to take entrance examinations, with the majority of Japanese students attending *juku* at some point during their education (Lowe, 2015).

The school owner also decided to branch out into daytime adult eikaiwa classes in order to financially support the costs involved in setting up the *juku*'s English program, and to be able to hire and retain me as a teacher seeking full-time employment. This eikaiwa could be classified as a single-location eikaiwa (Makino, 2016) which are typically smaller and individually-owned.

At the time I began teaching in these contexts, I commenced study in an MA TESOL program. While I had several years of teaching experience and a post-graduate certificate in teaching English as a second language, I was aware of the need to continue to grow as a teaching professional by broadening my knowledge of effective teaching methodologies that would further benefit student learning. The opportunity to interact with fellow educators in a professional community of practice was also appealing as a means to inform and guide my teaching and strengthen my reflective skills.

Over the course of this journey, my experiences from undertaking the MA program while concurrently teaching in the private education market allowed me to take greater advantage of the affordances I was offered in both eikaiwa and *juku*, but also caused tensions due to constraints that I faced. This chapter will explore and compare the affordances and constraints in each teaching context and examine how they influenced my evolving identity as a professional teacher over time.

Eikaiwa as a leisure activity

Advertising material promoted the school's eikaiwa lessons as beginner level, occurring at a "relaxing time" during the day that *misesu* (married women) and retirees could easily attend. Lessons were described as ideally suited to people who wished to learn English as a hobby after retirement age, enjoyed travelling abroad, or wanted to make use of English for volunteering. It was mentioned that the "native teacher" would be "easy to understand" and lessons would "proceed at a slow pace". To add to this relaxing atmosphere, English could be "enjoyed" with "delicious tea" and "baked confectionery" served during lessons. This description supports Kubota's (2011) notion of the eikaiwa industry being based on "leisure and consumption", often perceived as "a type of leisure rather than an intellectual undertaking" (Makino, 2016, p. 5).

Most students were the target demographic of homemakers and retirees and primarily came to learn eikaiwa as a "casual leisure" activity where students attend for the enjoyment and pleasure of socialising with others (Kubota, 2011). Some retirees also attended in order to stay mentally active. While some students expressed clearer purposes for taking lessons such as to use English in various situations when travelling overseas or communicate with English speakers in their local community, they generally did not come in contact with English between weekly lessons.

Private eikaiwa and examination preparation lessons were also available with an advanced payment system where students bought lesson tickets with a sliding fee scale for larger quantities purchased. My lessons were 40 minutes while Japanese English teachers' lessons in the school were between 50 to 80 minutes for the same fee despite all teachers holding similar qualifications. This suggested that lessons taught by the "native teacher" were more valuable and reflected the ideology of native-speakerism often found in the eikaiwa industry, where native English-speaking teachers are seen as superior instructors and considered to provide greater benefits for learning English (Cater, 2017).

Freedom without structure in eikaiwa

Teacher freedom has been cited as an advantage of private eikaiwa teaching (Nagatomo, 2013), in contrast with the requirement to often follow a prescribed curriculum and teaching methods in chain eikaiwa (Taylor, 2017). For my eikaiwa lessons, I was afforded a great deal of freedom and control regarding curriculum and lesson content, allowing me complete teacher autonomy to plan lessons in a way I believed would support students' learning. At the same time, there was a complete lack of structure or thought put into lesson scheduling or establishing a curriculum by school management. This created a sometimes-hectic environment in which lesson planning and providing continuity in instruction became immensely challenging.

After the eikaiwa classes were advertised, the onus was placed on me to plan everything. The management's focus appeared to be on the profitability of the *juku* with eikaiwa being a means to support this, as opposed to the educational interests of students. I received minimal guidance but it was made clear I would need to conduct lessons in a way that could easily accommodate new students at any time. I was nervous and unsure of where to begin as in addition to my lack of experience in curriculum-planning, I had no idea what to expect regarding the number of students who would join lessons nor their language proficiency and learning needs, which made designing several syllabi in a short space of time virtually impossible. Therefore, as a starting point I decided to purchase a series of mainstream English as a foreign language (EFL) textbooks to give myself and prospective students an ongoing lesson structure.

Despite being advertised as "beginner eikaiwa", several students among the initial intake were not beginners. After trial lessons, students were put into classes on different days and times to create discrete levels. In the following months, more students joined and were placed into classes based on my recommendation and the times they were available. Additional weekly lessons had to be established over time to meet new students' availability and English proficiency.

Using textbooks presented a series of problems. Students were initially given the option of purchasing a textbook which most took up, so I felt obliged to primarily use the books during lessons. However, as new students could become a member of the classes at any time, several students joined after a significant portion of the textbooks had been covered, hence they could not be expected to buy a textbook. Furthermore, it soon became clear to me that not all textbook materials were suitable for the EFL context nor relevant to students' ages and learning needs. This issue was highlighted by a student who was particularly invested in his learning when he asked me about my future plans for his eikaiwa class as although he enjoyed learning, he felt the content of the book was not always beneficial in supporting his purposes for learning English.

As I continued to grow and gain confidence through my MA study and teaching experience, I found myself personalising lessons more, modifying textbook activities, and supplementing textbook materials to provide students with greater opportunities for interaction and negotiation of meaning. I was also influenced through learning about task-based language teaching and the field of pragmatics. This led me to introduce tasks to give students regular opportunities for free production, and to incorporate pragmatic-focused instruction on different language functions to which students responded positively. Additionally, having complete autonomy allowed me to keep lesson plans flexible so I could teach at the point of need. Students appreciated this and did not show concern when a planned lesson extended into the following week. Having control also allowed me the possibility to promote learner autonomy, in conflict with the typical leisure-oriented eikaiwa model, as I regularly encouraged students to self-reflect on their learning and express what they had learnt or achieved at the end of lessons.

Once classroom numbers settled, I aimed to provide students with greater input over lesson content and classroom procedures by asking about their purpose for attending eikaiwa and the situations they wanted to learn English for. This knowledge helped guide my lesson planning through selecting and creating materials that covered students' preferences as much as possible. Students also commented on their enjoyment of free conversation and desired more opportunities to do this, so it became a routine at the beginning of classes.

Despite having complete freedom, the lack of any formal curriculum or assessment and the ongoing nature of lessons continued to increase the complexity of my lesson planning. I endeavoured to provide as much continuity as possible but with no syllabi or class progression, I felt there was no end point in sight for myself or students. I suspect, however, that I was the only one concerned by this as there were never any complaints from students, perhaps because most had no expectations regarding their lessons.

Preparing teaching materials that I believed would help students learn required significant planning, but I faced time limitations, a previously identified tension for eikaiwa teachers (Hooper & Snyder, 2017; Nagatomo, 2013). Over time I began feeling that my lessons were becoming more scattershot with no continuity in lesson content from one week to the next. Depending on the time I had available, some classes would be based on a textbook while I created my own materials for others. I often took several textbooks home and looked through them while commuting to decide what to do for the following day's lessons, or in some cases the same day. While freedom afforded me the chance to meet students' learning needs, the time constraints and ongoing nature of the lessons regularly diminished my sense of satisfaction with lesson planning and undermined my perception of myself as a professional teacher.

The flexible scheduling of eikaiwa lessons provided convenience to students but was sometimes at the expense of their lesson continuity and my lesson planning. If students missed their own lesson, they could attend another as a make-up lesson. While I sometimes repeated lessons across different classes, each class proceeded at a different speed which meant students would often attend a lesson they had either already taken, would be repeated again in their regular class, or one at a level above or below their own. The flexibility to change lesson times meant students could inform the school of their planned absence up until the time of their class. Occasionally I would arrive before class only to learn certain students would be absent, sometimes rendering my lesson planning impractical.

Integrating new students also caused difficulty when accommodating learners with different proficiencies in the same class. On one occasion, a prospective student attended a trial lesson in a low-beginner class with a retiree who had very particular learning needs. Although I informed management of the inevitable mismatch which would create a situation less than ideal for effective learning, either for economic reasons or a lack of understanding of language learning I was requested to "teach to the trial student's level". On another occasion, a highly advanced student was placed in a weekly class with a lower-intermediate student. This resulted in the student with the lower ability feeling overwhelmed by the spoken fluency of his classmate and his own limited comprehension, which eventually led to him requesting to change classes. By this point the pretence of "beginner eikaiwa" as advertised by the school no longer existed.

Identifying spaces for autonomy between the constraints of *juku*

In contrast to the minimal concern for eikaiwa, there was a heavy investment by management in the *juku*'s English program, the primary focus of the school, with clear curricula, program aims and lesson cycles established by management and Japanese English teachers. The program's primary aim was to increase students' proficiency in the four skills to excel in entrance examinations. Further aims were for students to acquire "real English ability" to "express their opinion in the international community in the future" and "be able to understand an interlocutor's intention". It was marketed as an integration of "conventional English learning" with a Japanese English instructor and "practical English learning" with a native instructor. Each teacher taught half of an 80-minute lesson with two classes occurring simultaneously. Japanese English teachers typically used grammar-translation teaching methods for reading comprehension while I was required to focus on developing students' practical English ability through speaking and writing.

However, institutional constraints such as the curriculum as well as expectations of parents and the school owner limited my autonomy in teaching according to my beliefs and knowledge. I found myself questioning the value of the educational policies for student learning as my knowledge of second-language acquisition theories and effective teaching methodologies grew. When faced with wider constraints on student learning, Benson (2011) has stated that a teacher's role is to identify how these can be "mediated through their agency" (p. 189). Therefore, I endeavoured to negotiate the constraints by identifying spaces within them and shaping lessons in a way I believed would provide students with greater learning opportunities.

Lessons were based on reading passages for high school and university entrance examinations and English proficiency tests, while some classes also used grammatical syllabi with one or two grammatical items introduced every class. Students received an audio file of the reading passage that I had recorded and were asked to listen multiple times while reading the text to familiarise themselves with it for the following class, where I was expected to get students to practice speaking by reading aloud. The school owner believed this would allow the meaning of English sentences to be naturally acquired by students. While I believed it could help students' pronunciation and familiarity with English sounds, it was the owner's personal belief based on how they had learnt English, yet this was not grounded in theory. Additionally, I was aware that students' individual learning preferences can have an influence on their enjoyment of different learning methods (Rosenberg, 2013), hence the usefulness of the school's recommended technique likely varied among students.

Therefore, while still meeting lesson expectations, I aimed to enhance students' opportunities for output and interaction based on methodologies I had studied on my MA course. Instead of having students simply read the text aloud, I used activities such as running dictation and the read-and-look-up technique (Fanselow, 2018) to help students learn how to pause naturally and speak with understanding. In addition, I promoted pushed output (Swain, 2000), where learners are pushed to produce the target language to help them notice gaps in their language knowledge, by having students express their own thoughts regarding the passage topics and practice using their newly learnt vocabulary. For classes with grammatical syllabi, I endeavoured to introduce the functional use of grammar points through communicative activities that required information exchange and negotiation of meaning (Long, 1996), in which speakers use communication strategies to gain a clear understanding of one another.

It was often challenging to focus on developing students' "practical English learning" and meet the advertised aims of the program due to the short 40-minute window of weekly contact and the management requirement to primarily use the reading passages. Additionally, when teaching before the Japanese English teacher, I had to regularly assist with students' reading comprehension if they came to the lesson unfamiliar with the material. The difficulty level of some examination passages, often beyond the students' school grade and language proficiency and with a large amount of unknown vocabulary, was also challenging for them.

My growing knowledge of second language learning and teaching theories also made me conflicted about some curricular decisions which I believed led to limited retention of learning. One or two grammar points were introduced on a weekly basis with students often given worksheets with sentence-level exercises focusing on grammatical accuracy, either in class or as homework by the Japanese English teachers. While a grammar focus is beneficial in raising learners' awareness of grammatical features they may notice in meaning-focused input, the grammar points were generally not covered again in a single lesson cycle, and it has been suggested that learners cannot be expected to be immediately accurate with new grammar structures (Thornbury, 1999). Additionally, due to time constraints, using practice tasks for individual grammar points with a focus on meaning to develop fluency was restricted to a small part of one of my 40-minute lessons and any homework I provided. Younger students were also learning advanced grammatical structures that may have been outside their current developmental readiness.

Reading passages were only used for one week for most levels despite myself and my colleagues generally focusing on or often only managing to complete a small section of the texts. However, our "less is more" approach to teaching went against management beliefs and our requests to use longer passages across two weeks of classes were rejected.

Furthermore, as I was required to focus on output skills, I was limited in using input activities that could engage students with new language receptively to promote consciousness-raising before using production activities. The bottom-up approach used for reading comprehension also conflicted with my belief in developing top-down processing skills to give students additional reading strategies useful for examination purposes. To negotiate this constraint, when asked to examine the answers to questions that accompanied reading passages with students, I encouraged reading strategies such as skimming and scanning while explaining their benefits.

Among the *juku* constraints, homework was an aspect I initially had control over which gave me an opportunity to afford more autonomy to students. I was responsible for assigning writing homework and through conducting my own action research, I confirmed that students were satisfied with writing short compositions as practice for entrance examinations (MacDonald, 2017). Some students, however, asked for more practice writing sentences based on the vocabulary from reading passages so I then gave students the choice of doing this as part of their regular homework.

Towards the end of my tenure, however, this opportunity for control over homework became restricted. Some parents, an important stakeholder in their children's learning, expressed a wish for a greater focus on learning grammar, which could be attributed to the importance generally placed on this in *juku* for passing Japanese entrance examinations (Lowe, 2015). *Juku* management began providing additional grammar worksheets for homework in addition to what I assigned, which added to students' heavy workload within their already busy schedule. The completion rate of my homework then declined, possibly because some students and parents felt the homework assigned by Japanese teachers was more important and needed to be prioritised.

Tension due to a clash of organisational cultures in eikaiwa and *juku*

A common tension experienced by teachers in eikaiwa and *juku* is negative relationships with management, often leading to demotivation and discontent with the workplace environment (Bossaer, 2003; Hooper & Snyder, 2017; MacDonald, 2019; Nuske, 2014; Taylor, 2017). This can be attributed to contrasting educational and business interests, as well as culture conflicts between teachers and management who each have their own beliefs and values but fail to gain a mutual understanding of each other's viewpoints (Bossaer, 2003).

My beliefs and those of my teaching colleagues on effective teaching practices were constrained by such conflicts in our relationship with the school owner and management. This was due to what I perceived as a clash between the teachers' desire to work together in order to solve classroom issues and achieve our own pedagogical objectives, and the management's preference to make all decisions which considerably constrained teachers' freedom for individual decision making. There was a reluctance by teachers to approach the school owner due to a lack of communication and meetings, with requests and suggestions often going unanswered. This was illustrated in a mentoring session I conducted with a colleague where they identified a lack of communication with management as a dilemma that affected their motivation and other aspects of their teaching (MacDonald, 2019). While the management and owner understandably had economic concerns, there was resistance in allowing teachers to be involved in the decision-making process. Hence, I believe we were not provided with the authority to guide our own professional development.

One notable incident was when a request was made to the owner by teachers to hold a meeting together. We wished to convey what was happening "in the field" that affected our daily classroom practices with suggestions on what could make lessons work more effectively. An initial request was ignored and a later request resulted in the owner making it clear that all proposed meeting items were management issues in which discussion with teachers would not be the best way to make decisions. This response had a very negative effect on teachers' motivation. As we had worked hard to make the school a success, it felt like our perspectives and pedagogical concerns as teachers were deemed to be unimportant and our level of professionalism towards our jobs was not recognised.

Over the course of my employment, I felt that the school management treated Japanese co-workers more severely than myself as the only "native teacher", which may have been due to the desirability of employing a native English teacher long-term to support the marketing of the eikaiwa classes and the *juku*'s English program. In one instance, unjustified pressure was placed on a Japanese teaching colleague regarding the financial aspects of the school, in which they were required to prepare an explanation of how they themselves were more effective in their teaching position than others would be and how they could attract more students. A proposal was then made by the owner to the colleague to become involved with management functions of the school, suggesting they would need to do this if they wanted to share their views about classroom matters. It appeared that non-teaching staff may have felt their own identities were threatened resulting in a need to assume a position of power. The treatment of my co-worker, despite their integrity and concern for student learning, created another source of tension in the workplace environment.

Reflecting on my experience in the private education market

It is important to mention my experiences in eikaiwa and *juku* are not generalisable to these industries as a whole and may significantly differ from other educators. As noted by Makino (2016), different types of eikaiwa can be distinguished by factors such as hiring practices, teaching practices, standardisation of teaching methodologies and materials, scheduling, and the target students. Additionally, although minimal research has been undertaken on English language teaching in *juku*, differences in teaching methodologies and materials could be expected due to the large size and absence of official oversight of the *juku* sector (Lowe, 2015).

Upon leaving the eikaiwa and *juku*, I was somewhat demotivated and burnt out due to the tensions and conflicts I had faced. I also felt a sense of being undervalued as I was barely acknowledged for my efforts. I did not, however, feel frustrated or disillusioned about teaching as reported by some eikaiwa teachers (Nuske, 2014; Taylor, 2017). Rather, I believe dealing with the constraints I faced and identifying the affordances available for student learning while still meeting institutional requirements assisted me in developing an awareness of my own beliefs and values of positive teaching practices. Undertaking an MA program where I was part of a professional community allowed me to justify my actions in terms of supporting student learning. Teaching in these contexts had a strong influence in developing my identity as a professional educator and will continue to influence my teaching practices going forward. I hope that other teachers in these contexts, where the conflict of interest between business and educational concerns can lead to tension and issues, will be empowered to analyse their own teaching practices, and reflect on and take advantage of any opportunities for affordances within the constraints that they identify.

Part 3: Professional identity and growth

11. The interaction of training and observation in one teacher's development

Marc Jones

This chapter began as a comment at a conference to one of the editors, where I remarked of the teachers present, "We are the freaks who give up our Sunday to sit in a university classroom and talk about work!" How did I reach the stage where I voluntarily attended a teaching conference on my day off? I had experienced a trajectory from enthusiastic, to satisfied, to frustrated with my career. It was in this state of frustration that I reflected on the root cause and realised that I felt compelled to develop my skills much further to continue in my career, which I had previously enjoyed and intended to continue. It was initially the lack of explicit development opportunities and investment in professional development by the eikaiwa companies I had worked for that frustrated me. However, in spite of the limited development opportunities, I improved my practice by implicitly learning from other teachers.

I eventually improved as a teacher but how I did so was not clear to me at the time. In this chapter, I shall explain the professional development affordances available through training and observation while I was a private language school teacher in the suburbs of Tokyo. Using personal experience of events to write about practices within the profession (Rodriguez, Shofer, Harter, & Clark, 2017) allows me to "foreground dialogue, incompleteness, the impossibility of separating or collapsing life from/into texts" (Adams, Jones, & Ellis, 2015, p. 10). This means that my personal experiences emphasised in this chapter are from my point of view. Any conversation excerpts are my recollection and may be biased or limited by my own memory. In other words, I endeavour to tell the truth, although it is a subjective truth.

Training

Upon arrival in Japan in 2003 for my first stint as an eikaiwa teacher, I was enthusiastic; I had a new home, a new job, and a goal of studying Japanese in my spare time. However, on-the-job training (OJT) five days after landing was a rude awakening. I was given a binder of pages from a textbook then told to pick out a language point and plan backwards. I was one of the least able trainees in my group and by the afternoon I wondered whether I had made a mistake. The problem was not the training, but the overall system of minimal instruction to create a minimum viable lesson and then learning to teach paying students by trial and error. If I had been required to take a TEFL course I would have had four weeks to gain the knowledge required to teach a rudimentary lesson. My company rushed through it in three days of OJT. By keeping training expenses low this was beneficial to the company, but it was stressful for me, and probably annoying for the students subjected to my early lessons.

In both of the companies I worked for, the classroom environments were, with few exceptions, either glass cubicles or open-plan rooms of tables, with up to nine chairs. This arrangement functions as a panopticon (Foucault, 1977), which "makes it possible to observe performances (without there being any imitation or copying), to map aptitudes, to assess characters, to draw up rigorous classifications" (p. 203). In addition, due to the materials used for the cubicles, voices in adjacent classrooms could be heard clearly. This panopticon allows those outside to look and listen inward, and those inside to look and listen outward. Although the primary reason was supervisory convenience, as a previous manager informed me, in contrast to Foucault's (1977) assertion that it would be "without there being any imitation or copying" (p. 203), it provided affordances for my colleagues and I to observe one another ad-hoc. This panopticon experience meant neither successful nor unsuccessful teaching could be conducted in hiding; this provided the impetus of staff room conversations, leading to informal teacher development, meaning that both successes as well as failures informed the classroom practices of my colleagues and I.

One month after my initial training, I attended a further one-day session where I learned games to play with children and was encouraged to feel less self-conscious. Once back in the school, colleagues as well as students could see everything so it was impossible not to feel self-conscious. One example was when a urologist, whom I would help prepare a presentation for an international conference in the next lesson period, witnessed me dancing and chanting "What colour is it? It's blue! It's blue!" while a pre-school child ran in the aisle between the cubicle classrooms, unconcerned by colours, English, and also me. While personally embarrassing, students occasionally commented on such occurrences. "I don't think I could be that enthusiastic," one female student remarked. Unfortunately, I rarely felt like enthusiasm compensated for lack of pedagogical knowledge.

Due to the panopticon, teaching was mediated through collegial discussion about incidental, informal observations with colleagues who commented on struggles, particularly where they lay in direct contradiction to training. In this particular school, I learned a lot from Andrew and Tom, as well as Gary, all teachers within their first year of joining the company. Andrew was skilled at teaching young learners. He also had a strong rapport with the teacher in charge of coordinating young learner materials and activities in our school, who had quite different working hours to me. As Andrew became her de-facto deputy, and my schedule was so similar to his, I had ample opportunity to take lesson ideas from him and therefore indirectly from the young learners coordinator.

Much of the practice that teachers engaged in at the first school I worked at was co-constructed by trainers, more senior colleagues and ourselves, through a mixture of advice regarding what works and what doesn't work. This was built upon with observations, which are discussed below. It is important to remember that in language teaching, knowledge transmitted in training does not occur in a vacuum but interacts with the practices of the trainees and their colleagues; it may also be assimilated to certain degrees or even outright rejected as unworkable or not worthwhile.

My training experiences provide examples of the realistic language school environment at the start of my career. I was required to teach according to a provided textbook in order to provide student (customer) satisfaction. I was thus reduced to what Gray and Block (2012) term a "skilled technician" (p. 119), in this case delivering behaviourist pattern practice rather than using expert knowledge to provide theoretically sound teaching and learning experiences. I was not guided toward providing exceptional lessons but providing sufficient opportunity for students to practice speaking. This view of the "skilled technician" is brought down further by Woods (1996), who states:

> The traditional thinking (as evidenced in audio-lingual methods) is that the learners know neither the target language nor the ways of learning it. The teacher, meanwhile, is considered to know the language (or at least be able to

demonstrate it), but not to know the way that it is to be learned or taught. (p. 189)

This lack of knowledge then goes on to make English teaching menial work. An analogy may be made with automobile production, where the work of highly-skilled engineers gave way to specialised but menial production line work. The way to teach and learn was provided, initially at least, by centralised OJT and follow-up training and workshops. However, bearing in mind that trainers in most eikaiwa schools are promoted from within the teaching staff, and mostly have no qualifications higher than certificate level, this can lead to practices remaining unquestioned and being perpetuated regardless of efficiency.

Such evolution from a skilled worker base carries on to formal teacher development. Gray and Block (2012) have stated that the neoliberalisation of education in Britain has given rise to a situation where "teacher education is set to be transferred to schools away from universities" (p. 121). However, in eikaiwa, this is taken further with English language teaching qualifications regarded as an irrelevance by the market-leading eikaiwa schools. Furthermore, language schools that are also certificate course providers still accept teachers without teaching qualifications. Both eikaiwa companies that I worked for paid around ¥5,000 extra per month for teaching qualifications. Unfortunately, any difference between a certificate, diploma, master's degree or teaching qualification was unrecognised. Teacher education was absent, with OJT the preferred mode of guidance, followed by very occasional short workshops. Unfortunately, these interventions did not always address teachers' pedagogical concerns and were top-down from the central office as opposed to coming from the teachers themselves.

One colleague who previously worked in eikaiwa said, "You don't learn to cook haute cuisine at McDonalds; likewise, you don't learn to teach at eikaiwa." Personally, I disagree with the strength of the comment but I am sympathetic to the overall message. I found that teachers I worked with developed their skills *in spite* of the companies, and that finding pride in their work was a motivating factor in doing so. "Even if the nature of the job is not meaningful to an employee, aspects of the work can become more meaningful when the employee reformulates and transforms given tasks, relationships and roles" (Falout & Murphey, 2018, p. 225). That is, in spite of there being no onus upon the teachers, there was internal motivation to find meaning in and make the best of a situation which was not ideal. Some of this was trying new text-based activities, finding ways to facilitate greater learner autonomy or finding out about different methods and approaches. None of this was guided nor were books provided for professional development; teachers were sharing good practices between themselves and developing practices among themselves in order to mitigate the shortfalls in provided training.

Observation

Due to eikaiwa schools being businesses, customer satisfaction was prioritised over teaching quality, in my view. The main way that both of my companies conducted quality control measures was by teacher observation. This was required at least twice per year for my first company and once for the second, and more often if there were student complaints. Both companies used observation for performance management purposes (regarding contract renewal and possible wage rises). Though dreaded, these observations were the only continuing professional development explicitly made available to teachers other than branch workshops or rare centralised training. However, the formal observations for performance management were less constructive than collegial discussions in the staff room. There is also a factor that teachers, myself included, are conservative when a manager, who has little to do with the day-to-day teaching at their school, is observing. The observations at my companies were conducted using checklists that included items such as greeting students, teacher demeanour, and maintaining dress code, which were given perhaps greater importance than items such as presenting new language, conducting practice activities and facilitating student language production. It could be that observations were regarded negatively due to teachers generally prioritising teaching over customer service, while observers were required to prioritise the latter.

Post-observation, a meeting would be booked where teachers received feedback and advice from the observer, often in the form of a mini-workshop. These post-observation meetings between a supervisor or an area manager and the teacher had high stakes for teachers deciding to stay in Japan, due to performance-related pay rises and contract renewals being tied to the outcomes. Mostly, these meetings were problem-solving sessions akin to the type of problematising in Carr and Kemmis (1986), albeit with teachers encouraged to think about improving their performance in areas of the observation that scored low on the checklist criteria rather than maximising the learning affordances of students. While teachers are situated in and reacting to their classroom experience during such problematising, they construct a truth based upon their point of view, while the observer does the same albeit at a distance. As Kumaravadivelu (2012) states, "Teachers' identity formation, then, resides largely in how they make sense of the contemporary realities, and how they negotiate contradictory expectations, and how they derive meaning out of a seemingly chaotic environment" (p. 58). Therefore, post-observation meetings, where teachers negotiate the truth of their experience with observers, has the potential to disrupt their teacher identities, either beneficially or detrimentally.

Schön (1983) asks "Is professional knowledge adequate to fulfil the espoused purposes of the professions? Is it sufficient to meet the societal demands which the professions have helped to create?" (p. 13/374). The question is still apt. To what extent are these supervisor observations and the attendant feedback sessions fit for purpose, especially given the potential for identity disruption? Based upon my experience, it is of variable quality. As previously stated, most managerial staff do not have teaching qualifications and rely only on their experience and beliefs regarding good teaching.

In the second company I worked for, one of the Young Learner trainers conducted an observation on one of my classes made up of four boys aged six and seven. It was a successful lesson in my opinion, with all of the boys participating in the games in order to practice language necessary to complete a question and answer activity at the end of the lesson. In the observation feedback, I had scored excellent or good in all sections. However, the target for development (have learners repeat teacher instructions more often) felt arbitrary and simply like a requirement for the Young Learner trainer to complete for his line manager rather than something that actually required attention.

My feelings toward this development target tainted my working towards it; I did work towards it but it was a case of paying lip service to it rather than having an intrinsic motivation to do so. Instead, with the same class, I worked toward solving a problem of how to maintain positive affect among losing players of games in the classroom. A way around this was found by talking to another teacher and making the losing player the referee (or "boss" as I had termed it) in following game rounds, or choosing whether they went first or last.

While the formal observations mandated for performance management facilitated development with extrinsic motivation due to a feeling of requirement, in the panopticon environment described previously, it was possible to conduct informal peer observations. These were a rewarding form of CPD, because context-relevant information as well as feedback could be collected and self-awareness of one's own teaching could be developed (Richards & Farrell, 2005. p. 87). Such observations may also take place without dialogue between observer and observed teacher due to time constraints or even simply forgetting to discuss something due to the movement in the teacher's room during breaks. It is therefore low stakes and lessens the chance of losing face.

Tom, a teacher that started working at my first company a few months earlier than me, was skilled at mining the required textbook for useful language and keeping his lessons active. He moved seamlessly from an opening activity to using the book as a reading or listening activity to present language for controlled practice and then free practice. He kept his talk about the lesson to a minimum, but talked to his students, providing authentic communication. This was something I aspired to, and by analysing what went on in his lessons, led me to ask more questions in my own, and reducing my commentary about lesson staging by giving simple instructions for activities.

Conversely, Gary, who arrived around one month later, taught middle-aged and elderly housewives slang such as "sick" and "off the hook." This led to overhearing scaffolded conversations about sick ballet and how a classic melodrama DVD was off the hook according to two ladies in an intermediate lesson. Because not all teachers are brilliant, observations can provide negative evidence of good practice. The way that students continued through the lesson, repeating the slang items in controlled practice and attempting them in free practice was so distracting from the task of monitoring my own students I remember it vividly sixteen years on.

I feel there are two distinct ways that observations such as these have influenced my teaching. The first is more predictable in that seeing effective classroom practice and mimicking it makes for practice to build skill development. Additionally, being observed and questioned about my own practices afforded an opportunity to reflect with greater purpose because not only my practice or my colleagues' practice was at stake but also the learners' instruction.

The other way is by seeing ideas fail in the classroom I could usually understand why and how they failed and decide to use the activities with adaptations in order to avoid problems, or to outright reject them as unworkable. This tended to work better with casual observations of regular instructors rather than those in management positions giving a formal workshop, perhaps due to seeing the activity taking place in a lesson with actual students rather than with teachers roleplaying as students.

Conclusion

Within the training and observation during my time as a teacher in chain eikaiwa schools, there were some experiences that were explicitly intended to provide influence on my pedagogy, although casual observation experiences and collegiate conversations between lessons provided more long-term impact. While I am not stating that this is the universal eikaiwa teacher experience, it was possible for me to develop as a teacher in spite of the limitations of corporate eikaiwa that lack CPD programmes and access to forms of teacher education beyond centralised training sessions.

Overall, casual observation has allowed me to synthesise ideas taken from others, though those ideas have been reflected upon and adapted for my own teaching style. Early in my career, I could discuss the ideas I took away with the teachers directly, and see how they worked in context. In fact, because these ideas were initially seen in a classroom context, they were already assessed as useful or else dismissed. This assessment and choice shows that teachers can exercise control over how they want to develop, and this freedom can lead to collegial discussions in staff rooms. At some point it may even lead to spending a weekend talking about work with other professionals in the teaching community.

My current professional development process is a more evolved version of my observation in the panopticon. Instead of limiting the community to the language school, the greater panopticon that social media provides allows an expanded commons from which to take ideas and engage in dialogue with the wider language-teaching community. I engage with practitioners on social media, read blogs, research papers and other professional publications; I take the ideas within, often in combination with my own ideas or those of others, to create something new to me. I also share my own ideas on social media and on my blog. While this use of others' ideas could lead to a lack of originality, I believe originality in teaching comes from a continued synthesis and re-synthesis of others' ideas along with my own. While it is not possible to see the initial ideas I take from social media in the classroom (because of issues regarding video recording one's classes and broadcasting on the internet), at the current stage of my career I know what is likely or unlikely to work in my classroom due to having amassed experience of evaluating activities seen in my colleagues' classrooms and reflecting upon them.

12. Context is everything: Qualifications, training and the myth of the untrained eikaiwa teacher

Luke Lawrence

Introduction

A few years ago, I was talking to a colleague who used to recruit for a large culture school and he was saying that he only used to hire ex-Akaiwa (a pseudonym for a large eikaiwa chain school in Japan) teachers because they were simply the best teachers. Then he added "I don't know what kind of training program they had going on there, but they were doing something right." At the time, this struck me, not because it went against my own beliefs and experiences (quite the contrary in fact, I had gone through the Akaiwa training and even been responsible for delivering part of it and think that it is a good program) but because it went against the wider narrative. This is the well-known and widely accepted belief that eikaiwa schools, and Akaiwa in particular, offer low-quality, pedagogically unsound classes taught by untrained and unqualified "backpacker" teachers. It was in this moment that I realised that not only had I been complicit in perpetuating this false grand narrative, but that I had also bought into the myth that the established industry qualifications such as CELTA and TESOL and even MA TESOL courses represented the pinnacle of modern training and that anyone who possessed one was bound to be a better teacher than someone who didn't.

In this chapter, I will use my own personal experiences of five years working in the eikaiwa industry as a teacher and manager as well as 5 years working in the university sector to explore the issue of training vs qualifications. In doing so I hope to deconstruct the myth of the "untrained" eikaiwa teacher and argue that context-dependent in-house training and job experience can often provide more practical and effective teaching skills than official qualifications.

CELTA/TESOL vs In-house training

In recent years, the standardised ELT qualifications of CELTA and CertTESOL have come under criticism for failing to meet the needs and expectations of "non-native" speaker teachers (Anderson, 2016; Lowe & Lawrence, 2018; McBeath, 2017), but I would extend this to cover any teacher not working in a multilingual context in the home country of the L1, i.e. most ELT teachers in the world, whether they are a "non-native" speaker or not.

When I started teaching at eikaiwa in July 2002, fresh off the back of completing a CELTA course in the UK, I was pretty surprised, and somewhat proud of the fact that I seemed to be the only person in my training group with this qualification. As I went through the pretty thorough in-house training I approached it with a certain arrogance, often taking the lead in sessions and being the first to offer up my ideas and opinions for lesson-planning. I didn't quite see the other trainees as know-nothing, non-serious "backpacker" teachers at that stage (that would come later) because I hadn't yet heard about the concept, but I definitely remember feeling that my CELTA had given me a head start over the other trainees and that the job was going to be easy for me, at least compared to other teachers. As a consequence of this self-assuredness, I patiently sat through the training, but silently rejected out of hand anything that didn't chime with my CELTA training.

As soon as we got into the practical on-the-job training (OJT) part of the training course, I realised that I was in way over my head and that the CELTA wasn't going to be much help at all. In my very first OJT lesson, which I had planned meticulously, largely disregarding the in-house methodology and using what I had learned from my CELTA training, I had one of the worst teaching experiences of my life. What was supposed to be a group of four students turned out to be only one student (what was known as a 'lucky man-to-man' lesson). I raced through my entire 40-minute lesson plan, which was based entirely on group work, in under 15 minutes and myself and the student sat looking at each other awkwardly in a tiny booth for what seemed like a very long time. My CELTA training had taught me to deal with groups of around 15-20 students, I thought I could just about adapt that to four students, but certainly not to one. If I had taken on board the in-house training more, which had a built-in flexibility to adapt to different numbers of students, I might have done a better job. The "'one-size-fits-all' approach" (McBeath, 2017, p. 249) of CELTA had failed me for the first time, but certainly not the last.

My next realisation of the fallibility of what I had learned on the CELTA course came from my approach to TTT (teacher talk time). Throughout the whole of my CELTA training I had it drummed into me, almost like a mantra, that high TTT was bad and low TTT was good. This even formed part of the assessment criteria, punishing anyone who deviated from this supposedly self-evident path. I had taken this 'truth' to heart to such an extent that I tried every sort of trick I could think of—gestures, pictures, charades, peer correction—to avoid actually talking. But as pointed out elsewhere (see Lowe, this volume), eikaiwa is a unique kind of language class and the teacher talking is one of the main ingredients. By taking an eikaiwa class, students are not only learning English, they are buying a cultural experience (Kubota, 2011a), which very much includes communicating directly with the teacher as well as other students in the small group. By keeping TTT low I was not being a "good" teacher in the context of eikaiwa. At the time (and for many years after), I used to sneer at the teachers that I heard through the glass of the booth who seemed to love the sound of their voices, and I couldn't understand how they got such good feedback from students – I knew I was a better teacher than them, I had a CELTA to prove it! It is only with hindsight and after a long period of critical academic study that I now realise that I was wrong. What I saw as high TTT "Charisma Man" (Rodney & Garscadden, 2002) teaching and lack of pedagogical rigour (see Hooper, Oka, & Yamazawa, 2020 for a nuanced appraisal of "native" and "non-native" speaker roles in eikaiwa) was in fact teachers following the training they had been given, which advocated using the teachers own background knowledge and culture as the basis for lesson planning and delivery of language teaching.

The final failing of my CELTA training was its lack of adaptability to new circumstances and new ideas. A couple of years into my eikaiwa career, a company-wide decision was made to switch from lessons based around discrete grammar points (as my CELTA course also had been) to a task-based one. In order to deliver this, new in-house textbooks were introduced and all lessons came with a Lesson Management Plan (LMP) with suggested activities to do at each stage of the lesson. All teachers were given new training in this system and as I was a manager by this point I was asked to deliver some of the training in my own branch. For the first time since I had undergone the CELTA training I found myself finally breaking free from it, and not uncoincidentally, for the first time in my career I found myself becoming a better teacher.

This transformation had little connection with the change from grammar-based to task-based lessons and the LMPs were not completely responsible either, it was just the first time that I had taken account of the context that I was in and due to the fact that I was a trainer, it was the first time that I had paid full attention to the training I had been given. The new textbooks had been developed by the company and were therefore tailor-made for Japanese students studying in a small-group, eikaiwa context. The suggested activities were also made for small-group work with built-in flexibility to adapt to "man-to-man" classes and were geared towards the specific demands of eikaiwa students. As I was delivering the training I began to realise the value of it and started to see all the parts I had ignored before. This feeling was strengthened by a number of follow-up workshops (created and delivered by myself and other teachers) and teacher evaluation sessions that really gave me the confidence I needed not only to become a better teacher, but to become ME as a teacher, to break out of the CELTA mould that I had been cast in. In some ways, I don't think I ever have broken out of the mould completely, and even went back into it to some extent in my post-eikaiwa career (see Lowe & Lawrence, 2018 for a fuller exploration of this). As counter-intuitive as it sounds, by taking on board a well-developed systematic training methodology I was finally able to develop my own teaching style that suited both me and the students I was teaching.

Eikaiwa training vs university qualifications

A few years after my time working at an eikaiwa had come to an end, I found myself working at a reputable English school in Tokyo, a position I was only able to get due to my possessing a CELTA. One day I was talking to a friend in the office and he nonchalantly mentioned that he had just started a master's course in TESOL and Applied Linguistics by distance learning from a university in the UK. I was awestruck. I couldn't believe that normal people could just casually start such a lofty and impressive undertaking. I asked him which university he was doing it at and went home and immediately applied for the same course. I threw myself into my studies with enthusiasm and excitement. I loved every part of it: the reading, the essays, thinking deeply about things that were interesting to me. I remember being a bit surprised that it was all theory and no practice (Papageorgiou, Copland, Viana, Bowker, & Moran, 2019), but I saw this as a good thing. I arrogantly saw myself as being beyond the need for practical application of my studies. In my mind, practical stuff was for the likes of (what I saw as) lower status Diploma (DELTA/DipTESOL) students. By that time I had 10 years' teaching experience, which I thought would make me an expert. Yet again I had failed to consider the context of my teaching situation.

A little time after completing my master's I started working full-time at a university and I felt like I had finally made it. The narrative that I constructed for myself was that I had worked hard, started at the bottom (eikaiwa) and worked my way up to the top, in terms of job status as an English teacher in Japan (Nagatomo, 2012). Like the participants in Appleby's (2014b) study of white Western men working in Japanese higher education, I was very keen to emphasise my academic credentials and distance myself from the "unqualified losers" I had left "behind" in eikaiwa. I was sure that universities were the places where the "real" teaching and learning happened and I had my newly-minted master's degree to help me do it.

As before, I found that things were not exactly as I had anticipated and once again it was my prestigious official qualification that let me down. In their study of UK ELT master's courses, Papageorgiou et al. (2019) found that only 34 out of 141 courses offered practical teaching experience and only 12 provided "microteaching" – simulated practice with peers as students. Results from focus groups and questionnaires suggested that students regarded practical teaching as an important aspect of their master's courses and that not enough of the course time was spent on practical aspects. This is definitely true of my experience too. Although at the time I thought that I was beyond the need for practical teaching training, when I found myself alone with several large classes of first and second-year university undergraduates, a series of compulsory textbooks and no support from the department about how to actually teach (I had an MA, so they presumed that I should know!), I realised that I was in trouble (again!).

In those difficult first weeks and months, my initial reaction was to throw off what I had learned from my master's and revert back to the good old PPP, discrete item lesson focus of my CELTA training. On paper my classes were closer to the classes I had taught in my practical lessons on the CELTA course – large groups (16 to 24 students per class), young adults, pre-intermediate language level. However, once again, I found that coming to terms with the context was the key (Holliday, 1994). The fact that all of the students shared the same L1 and were enrolled in compulsory English classes that they were required to pass in order to graduate from university, presented the two biggest challenges. The CELTA had given me no training in how to deal with monolingual classrooms and, still brainwashed by the English-only ideology that the CELTA had ingrained in me, I seemed to spend half of the lesson time telling my students to stop speaking Japanese and to stick rigidly to English-only. The rest of my energy was taken up trying to keep the students interested and motivated, something that had not been a problem in my CELTA training as the students had invested a great deal of money to come all the way to the UK and were therefore highly motivated to improve their English. Similarly, when working in eikaiwa, the students had paid a lot of money, often taking out loans and putting themselves in financial difficulty in order to learn English, making for highly motivated classes.

With my CELTA training being little help, I turned to the theoretical underpinnings of my MA studies. I re-read the modules I had studied on Second Language Acquisition (SLA), CLT, the various "approaches" of the 80s and 90s, as well as the small amount of literature on motivation that the course had covered. Chomsky's (1965) theory of Universal Grammar proved even more pointless in reality than it had sounded on paper ("theoretical linguist" is surely an oxymoron!), Krashen's (1985) Input Hypothesis didn't make much sense with the limited class time my students had for English lessons, and Long's (1996) Interaction hypothesis failed at the first hurdle when I realised that there was no need for negotiation of meaning when everyone shared the same L1 and to artificially force it would only antagonise my students and reveal the sham behind what were supposed to be meaningful exercises. I tried Lewis' (1993) Lexical Approach very briefly, before being limited by the textbook requirements and the apathy of the students. The literature on motivation was the most useful, although with the vast majority of my students falling under the "extrinsic" category of having to score over 500 on the TOEFL PBT, much of it proved irrelevant, or idealistic at best. In the end, I found the most useful academic contribution was the literature I read around group dynamics, which hadn't been covered by my MA course. Focusing on improving the whole-group cohesion of my classes allowed me to establish a base of engaged learners with which implement the teaching methodologies I was experimenting with (see Lawrence, 2017a, 2017b).

After four years teaching at the university, I feel that I'm finally finding my feet. I now have a decent grasp of what works and what doesn't, I'm finally happy with the balance of academic skills and language learning, the students are motivated and engaged (for the most part), and for the first time since the latter part of my eikaiwa career I feel satisfied with my own teaching. However, it took four years to get to this point and I can't help but feel that if I had had some meaningful, contextually relevant training when I started and at different stages along the way that I could have got to this point a lot earlier and a lot of students could have been spared directionless, below par lessons.

Final thoughts

After a long career, first as a CELTA student in the UK and then an English teacher in Japan, that has taken me from the tiny booths of eikaiwa to the conference rooms of international business, the crowded classrooms of public middle schools and the hallowed corridors of academia, I have had the opportunity to teach a wide range of students and learn a lot about my chosen craft. As I now embark on the ultimate academic journey as a PhD candidate, I find myself reflecting on the past 15-plus years and time and time again I find my mind wandering back to my formative eikaiwa experience. In terms of learning to think on my feet, planning and adapting lessons at a moment's notice and cutting straight to the heart of the matter to assess the needs of the students in a sentence or two, the experience was unrivalled. But it's not only that, the training that I received and helped deliver, that was context-dependent and based on the needs and demands of the students made me the best teacher version of myself that I could possibly be and in a lot of ways I think I've been trying to get back to that state ever since. No amount of academic study, official certificates or peer-reviewed publications has come close to making me the teacher I was back then and my greatest fear is that I'll never be that teacher again. I may have been less qualified, but I was definitely not untrained.

13. Two narratives of professional identity in eikaiwa

Patrick Kiernan

Introduction

Professional identity in eikaiwa, has sometimes been represented as something of an oxymoron. It is a theme that reverberates through such ironic depictions of the eikaiwa teacher in the *Charisma Man* comic series (Garscadden, 2002). In one scene, the eikaiwa teacher pretended that he was not a teacher in order to impress some girls that he met, only, to his chagrin and the girls' disgust, to give the game way when his textbooks fall out of his bag. The ambivalent social status of language teachers is also echoed in the teacher narratives included in Bueno and Cesar's (2003) book entitled "I wouldn't want anybody to know" after a teacher unwilling to share his experiences with the writers (p.15). The ambivalence of the professional identity of foreign English teachers in Japan echoes across the narratives in their book of those who did. Moreover, commercial eikaiwa schools, particularly the national chains that typically pay minimum wages, have been represented as prime examples of McDonaldization (Ritzer, 2000) offering "McEnglish for the masses" (McNeill, 2004) and poor working conditions to teachers. On the one hand, the rationalisation of the teaching curriculum and method, together with low pay and limited contracts, implicitly situates teachers socially alongside Uber drivers, delivery personnel, or convenience store employees as disposable cogs at the service end of a corporate machine. On the other, the eikaiwa teacher is interlinked with discourses of the "native English speaker" as either part of a hegemonic conspiracy of the English language (Kachru, 1990) or an object of exoticism and desire as a "Western Other" (Kelsky, 2001). The eikaiwa teacher, while seemingly benefitting from the myth of native speaker (Davies, 2003) and the prioritisation of English as a global lingua franca (Jenkins, 2007), in fact may lose their autonomy to Japanese corporations who profit from selling the services of these teachers to the public.

Although there may be reasons to be cynical about professional identities in eikaiwa or English teaching more generally, my experience of interviewing teachers about their professional experiences was that some teachers are more than willing to talk about their teaching openly. They also describe their experiences as rich and rewarding. Indeed, my own experience of teaching in eikaiwa over a period of 12 years while it involved negotiating these issues was extremely positive. Language school teaching gave me a rich and varied experience of teaching English as a foreign language. It enabled me to develop a sense of professional identity that, for example, stood me in good stead when I came to explore theoretical concerns when studying for academic qualifications. In turn, these qualifications have allowed me to legitimise my professional identity as a teacher and carve out a career in higher education in Japan. However, this chapter is not about my story but rather focuses on two narrative accounts of professional identity in English language schools in Japan, which nevertheless constitute distinct counterpoints to each other. It explores the ambitious career of Helen who came to Japan with the aim of developing her career as a teacher and did so through a specialized language school targeting high-level students. In contrast, it also considers the career of Graham, who came to Japan to marry his wife and initially knew nothing about eikaiwa but ultimately found himself well suited to the job because of his skill in handling people and a creative approach to teaching.

Narrative framings of professional identity

I regard identity as a slippery concept that has moved from being seen as a single unchanging self that can be dissected through such broad social categories as gender, class, and ethnicity (still used as key markers in quantitative surveys) to a position where identity has come to be regarded as something that evolves over the course of a lifetime, but also changes on a moment to moment basis in accordance with context. Consequently, I have come to view identity as multiple (Simon-Maeda, 2004), situationally dependent (Perkins & Thorns, 2012), and co-constructed in talk (Ochs & Capps, 2001). One effective way to explore professional identities is therefore through life history interviews where participants are encouraged to share their professional experience from past to present (a "macro-narrative") as well as focus on significant experiences through anecdotes (a "micro-narrative") (Riessman, 2001). Just as there is more than one way to tell a story, depending on perspective and context, narrative interviews should not be seen as definitive accounts, rather they make it possible to give voice to experiences and observations that might otherwise be overlooked.

The two interviews described below were carried out as part of a study into English teacher identity in Japan that included interviews with both Japanese and foreign teachers of English across a wide range of educational contexts (see Kiernan, 2010). These particular interviews were chosen for discussion in this chapter both because they were among a small number of eikaiwa school teachers who I had interviewed but also due to their complementary perspectives on professional identity. While one teacher framed her professional development as a career path that took her through the ranks of management to a position shaping the curriculum, the other explicitly avoided opportunities for promotion, because he saw this as a threat to his integrity as a teacher. The interviews themselves both lasted for approximately one hour. The first was conducted over the phone and the second face-to-face in the house of the teacher. The names used here are pseudonyms in order to retain anonymity. The interviews were audio recorded and transcribed in full.

An ambitious language school career

Helen's professional identity as a language school teacher was developed through a journey that began with a chance experience in Nepal but brought her to Tokyo for what turned out to be a challenging and rewarding career. Like many language school teachers, Helen's initial experience of teaching English in Nepal was undertaken in a casual spirit as a convenient way to fund her travels. However, when she returned to London, she was unable to find work related to her master's degree in Trade and Industrial Relations and decided to take the Royal Society of Arts (RSA) course (an intensive teaching qualification that was the most highly respected at the time) in the spirit of "Oh, well, I'll try this because I liked it." Likewise, she recalled: "I had a really good time on the course." This framing of her career choices as motivated by enjoyment was a recurring theme of her narrative. After working "with a great bunch of students" at a community centre in London she noted: "I started to get bored." Also, her choice of Japan was because "it seemed interesting and different" as well as offering opportunities for employment. She described her first job in Tokyo as "interesting at first" but quit because "you are very isolated, 'cause you rarely go into the office and rarely meet other teachers." Satisfaction in her job was therefore derived partly from the social relations with other teachers and her students. It was also related to her perceptions of movement in terms of her professional development.

Helen suggested that the boredom that she experienced at her job in London reflected the fact that this job did not contribute to the furthering her professional identity. She explained, "you really have to go abroad to move anywhere in the profession." thus aligning professional development with movement in the form of travel. For this reason, she described the London job as an experience where "You are just spinning your wheels really." Likewise, ironically, at her first job in Tokyo, she found that she was doing too much travelling that meant, "you end up spending as much time on the train as you do in the classroom." The long commutes constituted a waste of time compared to the worthwhile time teaching. In contrast to this, the job that she subsequently took was at a language school based in Tokyo that focused on teaching advanced learners including translators. Helen described it as a "good situation" that offered her the opportunity to move in terms of her professional identity:

> I kind of worked my way through the system. I started out as a full-time teacher, and then I er, became an assistant um, chief instructor and then chief instructor, and eventually I became director of studies there…I was ambitious, I wanted to move up, and I was interested in all different aspects of the job.

Summarising over ten years of experience at this particular school not only revealed her ambitious development as a teacher but marked the point at which she took control of her narrative, shifting to using "I" to indicate her own actions. This was in contrast to the more general "you" which she had used in the quotes above to characterise situations in which she found herself. Unfortunately, embezzlement by the school's chairman led to bankruptcy and new management prompted her to leave along with the "administrative level instructors." Though she said that she left on her own terms and was friendly with the new management who introduced her to the new company, she also pointed out that "they would probably have forced us out after they had learned what they needed to learn."

An important dimension of the knowledge that Helen and her colleagues brought with her to the new school was the ability to develop in-house "authentic materials from news sources." At her next school (which again specialised in teaching advanced learners) she explained, "they hired me to open the school basically." She described the new position as "a great job" where "I got to create the whole curriculum." Something that she did by bringing in "all my friends that I worked with [at the previous school]." More specifically she characterised the process of developing the curriculum as follows:

> …we took what we had learned…But since we were starting fresh … We could throw out all the things we didn't like, or things that we had seen wasn't working, or we weren't quite happy with… you know, we played around with things.

Once again, she used "I" to underline her autonomy in making the move but shifted to "we" to illustrate the collaborative (and social) nature of the project. An example of the specific problems with the curriculum at the previous school that they sought to address was "no information or guidelines on exactly how to use an article, so it was up to a teacher to decide what was appropriate, and how to structure the lesson." In addition to rationalising the curriculum in ways that potentially imposed greater structure on the classroom, and the use of written articles as source materials, Helen reconfigured traditional concerns of eikaiwa or "English conversation" in terms of "skill areas" which she described as "like how to organise your thoughts when you are going to speak in a formal situation, or how to give an opinion."

At the time of the interview, though still teaching at the school, Helen had relinquished her central role in the company after she became pregnant with her first child. As she spoke on the phone, her child played in front of her, occasionally demanding her attention. Helen's experience at small, specialised language schools oriented to an elite clientele of advanced learners is an impressive example of professional identity development in language school teaching in Japan because it was marked by progress through the ranks as her expertise developed and culminated in her effectively applying her knowledge to the founding of a new school. As such, she demonstrated considerable autonomy over her career and the career was one with features of promotion, training and management associated with conventional notions of professional identity. This is clearly different from the experience of many eikaiwa teachers who may struggle to achieve autonomy within the kind of large chain schools mentioned at the beginning of this chapter. For this reason, I was intrigued to hear the story of another teacher who had spent six years teaching English within the context of just such a school.

Eikaiwa at the bottom of the food chain

Graham had been teaching at a major eikaiwa school in Japan for six years when I interviewed him and was effectively settled in Japan, living with his daughter and Japanese wife who he had met in Australia. In many ways, the experience of eikaiwa teaching recounted by Graham, offers a remarkable counterpoint to Helen's description of teaching English in Japan, both in terms of the professional identity which he claimed for himself and the ways in which he evoked this identity. Whereas Helen came to Japan as a language teaching professional looking to develop her career, Graham did so without any knowledge of eikaiwa teaching and only taking up a post with some reluctance after other potential options failed to materialise. Conversely, while the school where Helen taught targeted an elite niche of advanced learners, Graham taught at a national chain catering to all learners but particularly those who learn English as a casual hobby or perhaps "serious leisure" (Hooper, 2019b). Moreover, while Helen progressed through the ranks of management to become the school director taking charge of the program and using her position in the new school to streamline the curriculum, Graham resisted promotion and the prescribed curriculum and disliked the suit and tie dress code imposed on him by the school. As such, he described himself as "at the bottom of the food chain" and represented his own perspective as at odds with the management, who in turn, he suggested were powerless to institute change in the context of a large national corporation.

Graham came to Japan with his Japanese fiancé who he had met in Australia without really having a clear idea of what he would do for work. They married soon after coming to Japan so that he was eligible to work on a spouse visa but did not do so immediately. As he explained, in Australia, he "was just doing this and that" which had included TV and film acting and reasoned that since he didn't speak Japanese, he needed to do something "that didn't require Japanese". Even when he found out about English teaching work, he was reluctant to apply at first because he "had never done anything like that before and just didn't know if he would be any good at it." He pointed out that he had never "gotten up and spoke in front of groups of people before." In the end, he decided to try after taking the advice of his wife's friend who had worked on the administration side of a language school. She persuaded him by saying that for him, "it is easy to get into. And the money's not bad. In fact, for what you do it's pretty good." The job began with three days of training in how to use the textbook and two months of probation during which he was frequently observed and provided with advice on how to teach. Nevertheless, apart from "the odd student who isn't quite what we expected", he described the job as "pretty straight forward."

Six years on, Graham remained in this position but also suggested that he and other "experienced teachers" ignored the specific lesson plans that were laid down by the school which he characterised as "a load of old rubbish." He explained that "It's all very set and, to be honest, apart from being excruciatingly boring to do it really isn't right for everybody" – by which he meant the students. In practice, he explained that "experienced" teachers "are very much left to do our own thing, except when we are observed once a year for the end of contract, so then you revert to doing it the [company] way." His description of the six prescribed lesson steps crammed into forty minutes suggests that the eikaiwa lesson had been over rationalised in exactly the way that Ritzer (2000) argued happens when corporations attempt to standardise their services across a chain or franchise of outlets. Just as the McDonald's hamburger must be cooked and served according to steps laid down in a manual, so the eikaiwa lesson had been broken down into a series of obligatory steps. While such predictability helps to ensure a uniform product it also suppresses human creativity and communication. The subversion of these practices in favour of more creative and individual ones (incidentally exactly what Ritzer recommended) ultimately helped make him a popular teacher among his students, arguably benefitting the company. Within the company hierarchy, Graham explained, the teachers were "regarded as the lowest of the low" (within the management hierarchy) with the foreign assistant trainers, trainers and head teachers above them and a separate hierarchy of Japanese staff beyond. Yet these experienced teachers like himself who "teach the lesson exactly as they feel like doing" are thereby positioned against those who follow the company methodology:

> Some of the people who have been promoted into training positions still do it the old way, because that is what they choose to do, or because they don't have the imagination to

do it any other way, or because that's, they are highly company motivated people.

Later, he pointed out that the "ones that are real sticklers for the company way" not only get promoted as trainers but "are generally disliked by the rest of the teaching staff." This may have been true of Helen who clearly aligned herself with her company and was successfully promoted. The school Helen worked at was clearly very different as she was given the job of developing the curriculum whereas, at Graham's school, as he put it, "any innovation is stomped on." In fact, when she came to start her own school, Helen suggested that one of the weaknesses with the previous school was that it lacked consistency and predictability because even though they drew from the same materials the activities were decided by the teachers making the curriculum "too diverse" so that "even though teachers liked it because they had a lot of freedom…it was too loose." Instead, she chose to orient the curriculum around functional skills, leaving the teachers free to select from a range of different materials (though not to use their own materials).

Despite different implicit positionings in relation to the company, a different style of language used to talk about the curriculum, and different language school settings, Graham and Helen actually seemed to be talking about similar methods and materials when it came to teaching advanced learners and showed similar respect for these students. Helen described her students as "smart people" and "mature" and Graham also talked of his students as "mature people with opinions and experiences." This is a reminder that they were generally teaching educated adults rather than children or university students taught by English teachers in traditional educational institutions. They also both mentioned the use of news articles used as the focus for discussions of current affairs. In terms of language goals too, Graham characterised the aim for advanced students as learning the way "you or I speak English rather than foreigners speak it" and getting students to express themselves in "good natural English" while Helen more specifically emphasised "how to organise your thoughts when you are going to speak in a formal situation." Likewise, when she described the kind of staff she wished to hire at the new school they sounded rather more like Graham than his managers "…we wanted people who wanted to do something more …we didn't want people who just wanted to open a textbook…And just …teach them a dialogue and ask questions."

While Graham had not had the opportunity to start his own school and underlined the impossibility of conveying his own insights to the school, he did run a remarkably successful class outside the corporation through a local community centre where he was free to teach in his own way which included not wearing a tie and being free to teach in the freer way that he preferred. Ultimately, he identified his professional success, particularly his popularity, as based on his ability to handle his students.

> I'm just very friendly with them all. I think that is all it is. I am very friendly and I make them laugh. I think if you are personable with them and make them laugh they will eat out of your hand basically.

Conclusion

This chapter has introduced the voices of two language school teachers in Japan who frame their experiences differently, but in complementary ways that help to make clear some of the prevalent issues of professional identities in eikaiwa. Both teachers frame their success in different ways. For Helen her success was described in terms of moving quickly through the system and company hierarchy and ultimately taking charge of the curriculum in the new school to shape it more effectively. In contrast, Graham was faced with an already over-rationalised system and a promotional system based around endorsing it. Instead he found ways to subvert it in order to teach in the way that he believed was appropriate. His professional identity was shaped both by his relative experience, use of common sense and a knowledge of how to handle people and a sense of his popularity as a teacher. For both these teachers, the teaching of advanced adult learners was regarded as particularly rewarding because of the opportunity to engage with other mature adults, something that may not be possible for those working with younger students in schools and universities. One thing that can be taken from the two accounts is that eikaiwa, though commercial institutions that are often used for short-term employment and may be endangered by bankruptcy on the one hand and over-rationalisation on the other, are also potentially rich sites for developing a sense of professional identity as a language teacher. As these accounts as well as those elsewhere in this volume illustrate, eikaiwa embraces a wide variety of school types and educational contexts that can lead to different discourses and formations of identity.

14. Charisma man or critical pedagogue? Eikaiwa and unexpected paths of professional development.

Kyle Nuske

Central Japan, spring 2007

I lingered awkwardly in the lobby of an eikaiwa school, a branch of one of Japan's major franchises, where I had just begun my teaching career. While my senior colleagues and long-time students joked with each other like the oldest of friends, I was acutely self-conscious, stumbling through exchanges as I inwardly succumbed to panic. In mere moments, I would have to attempt to teach an upper-level class for which I was woefully underprepared. I wanted to flee into my classroom and make one last frantic attempt to get a grasp on the textbook content and premade teaching materials that I would soon be expected to cobble together into a coherent lesson. However, teachers were expected to socialise with students during "lobby talk," the short intervals between lessons when new groups of learners arrived, so I remained put as the final seconds ticked away, numb to the lively chatter buzzing about my ears.

Once innocuous warm-up activities were completed and the lesson began in earnest, it spiralled toward failure with the grim inevitability of a Greek tragedy. Students struggled to grasp certain intricacies of the lesson target, distinguishing the past perfect and past perfect continuous tenses, and my desperately improvised explanations only seemed to plunge the class deeper into a mire of confusion. Yet, my pupils were sympathetic and gracious to the end – many of them had experienced similarly ineffective lessons from previous novices. They salvaged the class as best they could by taking the opportunity to practice general English conversation, though their good-natured perseverance only deepened my sense of shame.

I concluded the lesson in a daze, half-mumbling apologies while averting my students' eyes. Walking back into the lobby, I stopped and considered one of my employer's promotional posters hanging in the front window. It displayed a white male teacher (or, more likely, a model hired to portray one): young, attractive, immaculately dressed in business attire, and projecting a gentle warmth. In my own wrinkled, off-the-rack suit, my face betraying a long day's accumulation of nervous tension and fatigue, I could not help feeling like a rather shabby approximation of this perceived ideal.

Current vantage points and ambitions

In the course of my two-year tenure at a corporate eikaiwa school, I would come to interpret my teaching and workplace experiences (most of which were, thankfully, not nearly as disastrous as that described above) in terms of the corporate eikaiwa paradigm's larger structural characteristics and underlying ideologies. This process of reflection grew far more diverse and complex as I enrolled in a doctoral program in applied linguistics and TESOL at an American university, specialised in the topic of critical pedagogy for my dissertation and subsequent publications (e.g., Nuske, 2014, 2015, 2016, 2018, 2019), and was eventually hired as an assistant professor of English by a Japanese university. Given my critical orientation to research and practice in English language teaching (ELT), it is unsurprising that I now principally interpret eikaiwa chains as a manifestation of native-speaker supremacist ideologies, which construct and sustain hierarchies in access to teaching positions and their associated levels of power, prestige, and material compensation. To be clear, however, this general critique of one stratum of eikaiwa should not be indiscriminately extended to others, such as smaller, individually-owned schools, nor is it intended to suggest that higher education is devoid of native-speakerism or immune to the profit-minded machinations of neoliberalism (indeed, far from it.)

In addition to deliberately conflating the concept of teaching expertise with native speaker status, eikaiwa chains market their services by exploiting racialised discourses and images, such as those of the courteous and compassionate Caucasian male (Bailey, 2006; Kelsky, 2001; Takahashi, 2013), and promoting the value of English proficiency for achieving career mobility and stability in volatile labour markets (Nuske, 2019), a proposition that has been contradicted by empirical evidence in some cases (Kubota, 2011b). Put briefly, the problematic dimensions of eikaiwa chains are numerous and have been discussed in considerable detail.

Nevertheless, for all of my critical convictions, I cannot claim that my past experiences at eikaiwa hold significance only as point of departure and a representation of everything I now define myself against. Indeed, I find upon honest introspection that my earliest teaching efforts continue to influence my pedagogy and classroom persona in ways both subtle and overt. My intention for the remainder of this text, therefore, is not to merely indict eikaiwa, as has often been done before, but to retrace my journey through the highs and lows of eikaiwa teaching. Neither the nature of my experiences nor the critiques and observations I raise on the basis of them are wholly unique, but I hope to illuminate them vividly enough to prompt meaningful comparison and reflection among other scholar-practitioners. Moreover, I consider how my current teaching philosophies and approaches involve attempts to creatively and subversively repurpose tenets of the corporate eikaiwa method towards more critical ends.

Adventure and disillusionment: The journey begins

Though I wish I could begin my tale by describing a moment when I was suddenly struck by a noble inspiration to journey abroad, in truth my decision to move to Japan and become an eikaiwa teacher was born of an idle fascination, the lack of a larger purpose, and sheer random chance. In early 2007, I had completed a master's degree program in composition and rhetoric, but a teaching assistantship that was promised to me at the time of enrolment had failed to materialise. Lacking practical experience, I was unable to compete for suitable teaching positions after graduation, and I eventually found myself working full-time at a bookstore. After spending half a year adrift in this sea of inertia and malaise, I opened a newspaper and happened to see an advertisement with the tantalising heading "Teach English in Japan!"

A long-standing interest was reignited in that instant. As an abstract entity in my imagination, Japan had been alluring since my early childhood, when obsessions with Nintendo and Saturday morning monster movies took root. The appeal of Japanese popular culture intensified during my undergraduate studies as I grew enamoured of Japanese cinema and the work of canonical auteurs such as Yasujiro Ozu, Akira Kurosawa, and Kenji Mizoguchi. Eagerly copying down the job interview date and location, I was swept away by exoticised visions of striking angular shrine roofs and impossibly crowded neon cityscapes. My utter naïveté in regards to teaching English as a foreign language posed no deterrent – in fact, the ad reassured me that any sort of bachelor's degree was sufficient qualification.

Of course, many scholars have commented on eikaiwa franchises' tendency to devalue legitimate teaching expertise in favour of factors such as youth, demeanour, and appearance when making hiring decisions (e.g., Lai, 1999). Furthermore, some eikaiwa operators have confessed that their clientele prefers white teachers (Kubota, 2011a); when considered in tandem with the representational dominance of Caucasians among foreigners depicted in eikaiwa ads targeted at Japanese consumers (Bailey, 2006; Nuske, 2019), this disclosure raises questions about whether hiring practices are covertly influenced by racial biases. At the time, however, such concerns were foreign to me. I was enthralled by the prospect of adventure—an attitude encouraged by company recruiters throughout the interview process—and, once successfully hired, I journeyed abroad in the arrogant faith that my first language fluency in English would somehow see me through any difficulties that might arise in the classroom.

Upon arriving at a large city in central Japan and commencing a week of intensive training, I felt as if I were in the grips of a perpetual vertigo: in one moment, I was at the height of excitement amid a bustling urban sprawl; in the next, I was mired in the depths of jet-lagged exhaustion. For the next seven days, I would be inundated with a series of prescriptive routines—the only approximation of language teaching that the trainers could hope to impart within such a short time—and then shuttled off to my place of employment, a mid-sized suburban industrial town.

Though my employer's heavily standardised approach provided a psychological safety net during the most nerve-wracking nascent stages of my teaching career, I found that the array of drills and scripted activities with which I was equipped did little to prepare me for students' spontaneous questions and sudden difficulties, leading to frustrating and embarrassing failures in the classroom, as I have mentioned. Furthermore, my formal training in composition and rhetoric, which had centred on the teaching of rhetorical techniques and academic discourse conventions to native English-speaking undergraduates, seemed to have few meaningful applications in the eikaiwa domain.

As I became more comfortable with rudimentary aspects of teaching and began to seek out means of professional growth through self-directed study and informal consultations with peers, the regimented structures forced on me quickly grew constrictive; they provided a tenuous baseline of quality control but thwarted experimentation and diminished possibilities for the type of spontaneous, inspiration-based deviations from the norm during which the most substantive work of teaching is often performed. As such, brainstorming with Japanese and foreign colleagues about how to deliver better lessons was restricted to a slight and inefficient process of modifying imposed materials and procedures rather than crafting contextually optimal approaches from the ground up.

For these reasons, I have opposed blanket standardisation throughout the various contexts of my subsequent academic career, pushing instead for systems of mentoring, observation, and dialogue among autonomous professionals. I additionally invite my current students to question the relative merits and limitations of common standardised English exams in Japan, such as Eiken and TOEIC, encouraging them to think about how the abstract quantification of skills might be balanced with the establishment of self-determined and more personally fulfilling goals for language learning.

Eikaiwa as diverse contact zone

Whereas a lack of diversity, in the form of a rigid, deskilling system of teaching, was one of the worst aspects of my eikaiwa experiences, one of the best was the wide variety of students with whom I was able to interact: wizened and serene retirees, coolly brilliant automotive engineers, and bashful yet quietly exuberant office workers, to name only a few. To be sure, I am deeply fulfilled by my current university teaching and the opportunity to help nourish young people's hope for the future; however, there are distinct and equally valuable gains to be derived in classrooms where learners are of many ages, have traversed different life paths, and can speak to triumphs and tribulations related to full-time work, parenthood, aging, and so on.

In particular, two former eikaiwa students stand out in my memory as dignified, compassionate, and inspirational individuals who, at the risk of sounding trite, almost certainly taught me more in the course of our time together than I could have hoped to teach them. The first was a retired company executive who devoted the bulk of his time to volunteering and community service, specifically focusing on helping families provide terminally-ill elder relatives with home hospice care so as to spare the afflicted from passing in unfamiliar and indifferent hospital settings. Humbled by the nonchalant and self-effacing manner in which he described this work, I have since emphasised concerns of fundamental human dignity during classroom discussions of social issues, including Japan's rapidly aging society and resulting problems such as shortages of health care workers and the need for ethical immigration reform.

On a related note, the second inspirational figure was a Brazilian man who had immigrated to Japan with his family to perform factory work for one of the country's major auto manufacturers, which was headquartered nearby. Affable and already fluent in English and Japanese as well as his native Portuguese, he attended lessons simply to polish his conversational skills. Before and after classes, we spoke at length about his experiences as a member of the Brazilian immigrant labourer community. He was matter-of-fact yet unbowed as he reported how he and his compatriots were subjected to ritual exclusion and neglect, their presence treated with suspicion and thinly veiled contempt. His accounts made a lasting impression on me, and, upon returning to Japan years later in a context where I was afforded the autonomy to determine lesson topics, I eagerly sought out materials on the nation's marginalised minority groups.

In sum, emphasising humanistic dimensions of controversial topics and challenging the myth of Japan as an ethnically and linguistically homogeneous entity now rank among my most crucial and productive pursuits, and I owe these enrichments of my pedagogy to my former eikaiwa students, both of whom I would have been very unlikely to meet in more traditional educational settings.

Good times and false ideals

Another aspect of eikaiwa was opportunities for extracurricular socialisation, which to some students seemed to be of equal or greater importance than receiving classroom instruction (see also Kubota, 2011a). Unlike other corporate chains, which, according to testimonials posted on popular message boards for foreigners living in Japan, forbid teacher-student interactions outside of company grounds on the principle that any access to foreign instructors ought to be bought and paid for, my employer regularly organised group outings, including *nomikai* (drinking parties) for those of legal age. Truthfully, as a wide-eyed and uneasy neophyte, I relished these chances to engage with the host community and deepen friendships in heady and boisterous settings like *izakaya* (Japanese pubs/bars) and karaoke rooms.

Hence, I struggle to reconcile my commitment to tackling topics of substance in language education with these fond memories. More broadly, there is a need to acknowledge that, since eikaiwa participation is voluntary in most cases, students have the right to regard English as an incidental or frivolous aspect of their lives. If, as mentioned, some students persisted with their lessons for long periods despite exhibiting few signs of increased proficiency and prioritised leisurely conversation over rigorous study, this was ultimately their prerogative, and one which did not lessen the depth or legitimacy of the camaraderie we developed.

Nevertheless, in retrospect, I am given pause as I consider that these company-organised social outings may have been coordinated primarily as a marketing gesture – that is, in service of promoting a fantastical vision of English as the gateway to an enticing cosmopolitan community within the known comforts of students' home country (Kubota, 2011a; Seargeant, 2009). To reiterate, this fantasy is problematic in that many, if not most, of the individuals hired to populate the eikaiwa realm are from a narrow range of powerful, native-speaking nations. Thus, corporate eikaiwa's branded internationalism is one that belongs to a privileged elite and potentially renders learners unaware of, or indifferent to, the immense diversity of persons who fall under the broad categories of English speakers and capable language teachers.

As mentioned at the onset of this piece, eikaiwa franchises' marketing materials present even more idealised and exoticised representations of English teachers, extending beyond the general valorisation of whiteness and encompassing specific features of appearance and demeanour. (Although teachers of colour have sporadically appeared in eikaiwa franchises' more recent advertising materials, their inclusion remains slight and tokenistic—see also Nuske (2019).) The slender, clean-cut, compassionate, and chivalrous figures presented in eikaiwa ads often construct the image of a "charisma man:" an ordinary male who is magically transformed into an embodiment of Western refinement and sex appeal upon arriving in Japan (Rodney & Garscadden, 2002). Some male eikaiwa teachers enact charisma man personas by reciprocating the amorous infatuations of their female students (Appleby, 2013), and I indeed observed this phenomenon in practice when socialising with foreign teachers from other branch schools.

However, even before I began studying critical perspectives on ELT, I could sense that the single idealised identity into which all male foreign eikaiwa teachers were pigeonholed was far more alienating and repressive of individuality than advantageous. The obligation to exude an agreeable and easily-digestible "foreignness" may thwart practitioners' ambitions of implementing more sophisticated and intellectually demanding pedagogies (Appleby, 2013) or discourage them from using Japanese in personal and professional spheres (Takahashi, 2013).

Yet, for all of these misgivings, I find that the classroom personality I developed during my eikaiwa tenure remains an important part of my current teaching repertoire, albeit one that I now try to employ towards more subversive ends. In essence, by putting students at ease or even entertaining them with my upbeat and easy-going behaviour during early class sessions, I hope to build reserves of trust and goodwill that will facilitate genuine efforts when I later ask students to engage in various forms of critical inquiry, including the reconsideration of some fundamental assumptions about self, nation, and society. However, I must add that my ability to adopt this disposition remains rooted in my racial, linguistic, and gender-based privilege, in that I am not compelled to dispel initial doubts about my English-teaching qualifications as female and/or non-native speaking instructors might be due to prevalent prejudicial assumptions.

Endings: The bubble bursts

Despite some accumulation of frustrations and doubts during my first year of eikaiwa teaching, I felt my overall experiences and relationships with colleagues and management staff were positive enough to merit renewing my contract for another 12 months. Unbeknownst to me at that time, the 2008 recession would completely alter my workplace environment for the worse, bringing the most crassly commercialised elements of the corporate eikaiwa paradigm to the fore and replacing a relatively carefree environment with one of intimidation and coercion.

Put briefly, my employer's business model set monthly financial targets that each branch school endeavoured to meet by recruiting new students and persuading current students to enrol in further courses. Additionally, teachers were required during traditionally slow business periods to conduct individual "counselling" sessions with students. In actuality, these sessions consisted of sales pitches for supplementary study materials, which were soundly designed but grossly overpriced. Meeting the monthly targets through tuition fees alone rarely posed problems for our branch prior to the economic downturn, with the result that teachers and learners alike tended to dismiss the so-called counselling sessions as a nuisance to be conducted half-heartedly and soon forgotten.

After the recession hit, however, student enrolment decreased substantially, and falling short of the targets became the rule rather than the exception. As desperation mounted, our branch manager and her chief assistant began pressuring my Japanese teacher colleagues to convince students to renew their contracts and buy ancillary study tools, even scheduling multiple counselling sessions with particular students in a heavy-handed attempt to wear down resistance. (Once again, the limited Japanese proficiency of the foreign teachers amounted to a form of privilege, absolving them of such distasteful duties.)

Predictably, these schemes often backfired and caused Japanese teachers to lose students' trust through no fault of their own. Regardless, management ostracised them and imposed a litany of tyrannies both petty and profound as punishment for their poor sales performance. Disturbed and disgusted by the obvious psychological toll being inflicted on my Japanese counterparts, yet powerless to effect any meaningful change in the eikaiwa system, I resolved to quit eikaiwa work at the end of my contract and began researching doctoral programs in applied linguistics and TESOL.

Though I still cannot bring myself to forgive the management staff for their conduct, I now recognise that they were also beleaguered subjects of the neoliberal order, in many ways helpless against company directives and relentless drives toward maximisation of profit. I must also concede that I raised no serious objections to capitalist infiltrations of the teaching act until they began to disrupt my own routines of ease and enjoyment. Fresh contemplation of these developments suggests topics for critical inquiry in my future classes; for example, students could unpack the implications of the spread of Uber, a non-unionised, peer-to-peer transportation network, to Japan, weighing factors such as lower prices and increased convenience against longer-lasting consequences of neoliberalism, including reductions in permanent positions carrying health benefits and paying living wages along with workers' increased reliance on balancing multiple part-time and contingent positions for survival.

Final reflections

As I hope to have illuminated in this text, my earliest teaching experiences at an eikaiwa franchise continue to exert a powerful influence on my current critical teaching approaches, often in indirect and unexpected ways. For instance, they raised my awareness of the demographic diversity and social discrimination that exist behind Japan's veneer of homogeneity, shaped my classroom demeanour, which I now attempt to employ towards critical ends, and catalysed my belief that the essential objectives of education and business are incompatible to some degree. In closing, I wish to reemphasise that the corporate eikaiwa system does entail some distinct strong points—opportunities to interact with students from a wealth of different backgrounds chief among them—in addition to its many problematic dimensions and limitations. As such, I sincerely hope that eikaiwa business practices will be amended to help students and teachers achieve more productive and fulfilling classroom encounters.

15. Moving on: Life after eikaiwa

Andrew Boon

Introduction

It was roughly eight years ago when I answered a call for papers by Chris Stillwell (2013) to submit a book chapter for his upcoming title, *Language Teaching Insights from other Fields.* The premise of Stillwell's (2013) book was to bring together a number of language teachers who had started their careers in other fields. Stillwell (2013) asked each teacher to describe the knowledge, skills, and experience that they "regularly and naturally draw on" (p. 3) from their previous work backgrounds that inform their everyday teaching. After submitting my chapter on my experience of bartending and how the skills I had developed correlate to my actions in the language classroom (Boon, 2013), I became interested in the reverse of Stillwell's (2013) idea – what insights from language teaching do people who leave the profession take with them to their new fields? What skills developed by teachers in the language classroom are particularly useful in their subsequent occupations? As eikaiwa teaching has often been considered as an entry-level position (Hooper, 2018), with a high turnover rate (McNeill, 2004), I wanted to investigate people's (usually new university graduates) perceived value, if any, of the time they had spent working at conversation schools in Japan.

The current literature on eikaiwa tends to focus on the more negative aspects of workers' experiences such as the poor working conditions, (Currie-Robson, 2014), the lack of job security (Taylor, 2017), the over-commercialisation of eikaiwa education (McNeill, 2004), the struggles to develop and be recognised as a professional educator (Hooper & Snyder, 2017), the commodification of the 'native' language teacher (Kubota, 2011a) to such extent that in extreme cases employees can become victims of sexual harassment (McCrostie, 2014), and the general sense of eikaiwa teachers feeling undervalued, marginalised, frustrated, and demotivated (Taylor, 2017).

Despite the cons, however, not everybody goes through these issues and there can be many pros to working at an eikaiwa ("Zooming Japan," 2013). In order to address this, in this chapter I focus on the more positive aspects of the eikaiwa experience in light of it acting as a springboard to people's future careers. The chapter begins with my own experience of continuing in the field of language teaching post-eikaiwa moving on to work in tertiary education. I then examine the experiences of others who entered different fields of employment on leaving eikaiwa. I move on to describe the skills that they feel they gained whilst teaching in eikaiwa that were transferable to and useful in their subsequent or current positions.

Eikaiwa to university teaching: My experience

After completing my undergraduate degree and a Post-Graduate Certificate in Education (teaching certificate) in the United Kingdom, I got hired in London for an eikaiwa position in Tokyo. Unlike most of my fellow recruits who had taken the job to experience living and working abroad for a few years and then planned to return back to their home countries, I had a clear desire to become a language teacher and perceived eikaiwa as a good way into the vocation. The day after arriving in Japan, I was very much thrown in at the deep end – I had a full schedule of classes to teach including overtime work. Armed with my one 'introductions' lesson that I had prepared during the eikaiwa's very short pre-departure training, I realised it was very much sink or swim. The first few days of teaching went quickly - I gave my 'introductions' lessons to all of my students. However, it was soon time to prepare and teach the next set of classes. Thus, I had to learn quickly the importance of effective time management and of always being one step ahead with my lesson preparation.

As time went by, I became more familiar with using the coursebooks and the supplementary library of materials in the office and tried out different activities in my classes. I also became more reflective – I reflected-in-action (Schön, 1983) and became better at instinctively adapting my lessons to the ongoing needs of the learners. I also reflected-on-action (Schön, 1983) by considering what aspects had worked after each lesson, what had not worked, and what required further improvement. By doing this, I could implement relevant changes whilst developing my pedagogic 'bag of tricks' – activities that I could use at any given moment to help learners achieve the learning outcomes of a lesson.

Two years into my eikaiwa experience, I was offered the position of trainer for teachers who had decided to stay longer than a year with the company. The training involved participants examining a range of different teaching methodologies, trying methods out in their classes, reflecting on them, and reporting back in the following sessions. Not only did this role encourage me to read more in the field and become more theoretical, but it also gave me the opportunity to facilitate 'real' professional development sessions for my peers (other company sessions tended to focus on the 'teacher as salesperson' and strategies for encouraging student contract renewal).

Knowing that language teaching had become my true vocation, but wishing to move up the ELT career ladder, I decided to undertake a part-time distance-learning master's degree in TESOL. This had the dual advantage of increasing my pedagogical and theoretical knowledge whilst working towards attaining the qualification I needed to teach at the university level in Japan. Thus, I studied in the mornings before my eikaiwa shift began, in the late evenings, and on the weekends. After four years in eikaiwa and the near-completion of my master's degree, I could finally make the move and start teaching part-time at universities in Tokyo. After gaining more experience in tertiary education, publishing academic papers, and presenting my research, I was able to secure a three-year full-time contract position at a university which through hard work and recognition from senior faculty led to tenure.

Although the hours were long and unsociable, the pay was relatively low, and the company often prioritised sales over education, eikaiwa provided me with an ideal introduction to language teaching. It gave me practical experience in the classroom to develop as a teacher, the autonomy to develop my own lessons and materials (a plus of this particular eikaiwa chain), and an instilled belief in the importance of meeting learner needs. As my teaching career progressed and I met peers at academic conferences in Japan, I discovered that many of them had had similar beginnings – they had also started in eikaiwa. In this respect, eikaiwa can clearly provide people with an entry to and effective springboard for sustaining a career in language teaching. However, the focus of the remainder of the chapter will be the transferability of skills gained in eikaiwa by those who moved on to different occupations.

Eikaiwa to other fields: Other people's experiences

In order to collect data for this study, I posted a call for participants on my personal Facebook wall and on the wall of several teaching groups in Japan:

I am looking to interview 5 or 6 people who taught at eikaiwa in Japan and then went on to gain employment in a different industry. Namely, I am interested in the skills gained through teaching at eikaiwa and how they have helped the individual in their current profession. If you know of anybody who might be interested in being interviewed, please let me know. (A. Boon, personal communication, January 4, 2019)

I also privately contacted several peers that I knew met my stipulated criteria. I received positive responses from both current teachers and those who had moved away from the field. I was able to arrange interviews with 10 participants (see Table 1) and conducted the interviews via Skype over a two-week period in January 2019. Before each interview, I explained the purpose of the study, the intended publication, and I obtained permission to use interviewees' responses. Interviewees were asked the same four questions:

1. Which eikaiwa did you work for?
2. How long did you work there?
3. What jobs have you done since?
4. What skills gained while working in eikaiwa would you say were useful in your subsequent or current job(s)?

After permission was granted to do so by interviewees, interviews were recorded using the 'Voice Memos' iOS application. Interviewee stories were then analysed for significant categories (skills gained in eikaiwa) that emerged across the interviews.

Table 1 (p. 163) provides a brief description of the 10 interviewees. Interviewees have been assigned a pseudonym to ensure their anonymity. The table summarises the length of time each interviewee spent working for an eikaiwa and the jobs (or studies) they have done since leaving their positions in eikaiwa. Also, as three interviewees had returned to teaching after leaving the profession for a period of time, these data have been included in the table. Finally, it should be noted that as my first interview question (p. 162) was used only as a validity check to ensure participants had indeed worked for an eikaiwa, these data have not been included.

Table 1: Interviewee data

Interviewee	Time in eikaiwa	Job(s) / Post-graduate study after eikaiwa	Returned to teaching?
Peter	1.5 years	ALT work → Surveying equipment manufacturing company → Application engineer	No
Roger	2 years	ALT work → Language school & University teacher → Program development manager for cosmetics company	No
Matthew	4-5 years	ALT work → Started own photography and videography company	No
Paul	1 year	MBA → Starting analyst for a bank	Yes
Haruka	4 years	ELT consultant for bookstore and distributor	No
Miyuki	1 year	Secretary at NPO – soon promoted to head of the office.	Yes
Tara	1.5 years	Post-graduate study → Occupational therapist	No
James	7 years	Public relations officer at an embassy	Yes
Ken	10 years	Start-up Internet company → Vice Senior Manager of Back to Basics promotion office for Internet company	No
Lisa	3.5 years	National lottery - Funding officer → Corporate manager → University - Project management – Careers and Placement team	No

Transferable skills from eikaiwa to other fields

From the analysis of responses to interview question 4 (See above), eight skills emerged as being particularly useful in the interviewees' professions post-eikaiwa:

Time management

Time management can be described as the skill of planning one's time in order to make the most effective and productive use of it (Forsyth, 2007). For eikaiwa teachers, it is the ability to be organised, to have lesson plans and teaching materials prepared in advance, and to be ready for each day. It is the efficient use of any time that may become available whilst being aware that that time may be encroached upon at any given moment in the day by requests from the manager. It is also the skill of managing classroom time; helping learners towards achieving the lesson objectives within the allotted period of a class, being able to bring the lesson to an effective close, dealing with any remaining queries, whilst knowing that the next lesson of the day will soon begin, and the next set of learners are already waiting patiently in the school lobby for their teacher. Six interviewees stated that eikaiwa had taught them how to:

- work under pressure with a busy schedule (Peter & Lisa)
- juggle many different tasks at the same time (Roger)
- calculate when tasks will be finished and to work to these deadlines (Roger & Miyuki)
- be ready to deal with any unexpected work that may arise - "*to adapt to anything that came at me*" (James)

Several interviewees also mentioned how they had gained a deeper awareness of time and its value. Paul explained that he had become more "*mindful of time as it was passing,*" so that he would instinctively know when the start of a business meeting was approaching without the need for reminders. Moreover, he became more accustomed to dealing with the "*constant ebb and flow*" of the workplace with few opportunities to "*step back, reflect, and refine*" one's actions. James stated that he developed a deeper appreciation of the importance of other people's time so as not to keep people waiting or to keep them longer than they had expected.

Communication skills

One important characteristic of an effective language teacher is to have good interpersonal communication skills (Crookes, 2003). For eikaiwa teachers entering the classroom for the first time, there is an immediate need to transmit information via the L2 that is comprehensible, to modify one's lexis, rate of speech, and pronunciation according to the level of the students, to be able to elicit and make sense of students' responses, and to understand aspects and implications of Japanese nonverbal communication. Eight interviewees expressed their development of interpersonal and cross-cultural communication skills through eikaiwa teaching as being particularly important to them. Interviewees stated they had learned how to:

- adapt their communication to the person or people being addressed (Matthew, Paul, & Ken)
- relate to and interact successfully with Japanese in terms of social etiquette and customs (Matthew & Ken)
- read body language and know when understanding is not taking place (Tara & James)
- get the point across in engaging ways for a variety of different audiences (Lisa)

Interestingly, Tara described how as an occupational therapist she interacts daily with patients whose first language is not English or who have mental health issues. Due to her eikaiwa experience, rather than just "*repeat what I said and shout it louder*," she knows how to rephrase the language to facilitate comprehension. She also mentioned how eikaiwa had taught her more patience when interacting with others – "*You can't always be in such a hurry…you have to be more open to people not understanding you.*"

Mentoring skills

Mentoring has an essential role in business (Bartolome, 2017). It is a "learning partnership" (Eby, Rhodes, & Allen, 2010, p. 10) in which the more experienced worker or mentor can share their professional knowledge and skills with the new worker or mentee and give them guidance and advice. Here, there seems to be a close correlation between mentoring in the workplace and classroom teaching. For eikaiwa teachers, everyday activities are planning the best means to share one's knowledge of the English language, putting the plan into action in the classroom, and facilitating student learning. Moreover, the job often involves providing guidance to students regarding ways to study outside of the classroom. For more experienced teachers who take on positions as 'trainers' within an eikaiwa company, mentoring may involve helping new recruits adapt to their teaching role and become more familiar with different teaching methodologies, advising on classroom management techniques, as well as sharing strategies for increasing school sales with respect to student recruitment. Five interviewees stated they had developed mentoring skills via their eikaiwa experiences, especially how to:

- manage people, get the most out of them, and encourage them to listen and learn - "*get them enthusiastic*" (Peter & Lisa)
- understand what is useful for mentees to know and how best to scaffold learning into digestible segments (Matthew & Miyuki)
- empathise with or "*relate to newbies*" coming from overseas and adjusting to life in Japan (Ken)

Thinking on one's feet

Although teachers may plan their lessons, the act of teaching involves uncertainty, improvisation, and the ability to adapt lessons to the ongoing needs of the learners. Teachers learn to reflect-in-action (Schön, 1983); to think on their feet in the midst of teaching and make intuitive pedagogical decisions that may positively affect the outcome of a particular lesson. As with all teaching, eikaiwa teachers may deviate from their lesson plans to answer questions from students, to provide them with additional scaffolding or practice, to change their mood, or to adapt activities to fit the remaining time. Four interviewees described how the skill of reflecting-in-action traversed eikaiwa to their subsequent professions regarding:

- adaptability (Peter & James) - "*However much of a plan you've got, you have to be prepared to throw it all out of the window*" (Peter)
- dealing with problems as they arise in the workplace (Paul)
- using one's initiative to get the job done when little direction is provided (Miyuki)

Self-efficacy

Self-efficacy is an individual's perceived belief or judgment in their ability to perform certain actions effectively (Bandura, 1997).

Although not a skill per se, high self-efficacy can foster a desire for the individual to achieve greater goals, encounter more difficult challenges, and work continually on their professional and personal development (Noonan & Erikson, 2018). As eikaiwa teaching may be the first job after graduation for the individual teacher (Hooper, 2018), it can be the first step to developing confidence in their overall professional competence. Three interviewees stated that eikaiwa teaching had contributed to their self-efficacy in the respect of:

- building confidence – "*teaching is a performance*" that requires confidence; explaining or 'selling' the product to the customer requires the same confidence (Peter)
- building credibility when talking to teachers about ELT material due to prior teaching experience and background knowledge – "*I'm able to relate and it gives me confidence to be able to do my job properly*" (Haruka)
- enhancing one's self-belief - "*more confidence in myself and my ability to evaluate other people*" – especially, with regards to helping patients function in their daily lives. (Tara)

Selling skills

The duty of being a salesperson to facilitate the recruitment of new students and the continued enrolment of existing students is often seen as an unwelcome part of the job for the eikaiwa teacher (Taylor, 2017). Duarte (2018) argues, however, that there are many similarities between teaching and sales in respect of the need to provide unique customer care, develop professionally, keep up with change, work in a team, and be accountable for one's successes and failures. Three interviewees described their eikaiwa experience as useful for developing skills related to selling in respect of:

- understanding the need to believe in the product in order to sell it (Peter)
- taking ownership for one's actions, providing excellent customer care, providing value for money - "*making sure what I did contributed to the success of the team…or I felt I wasn't earning my keep*" (James)

- being able to sell oneself in a job interview to help secure employment by using examples of her successful student renewal rates at the eikaiwa (Lisa)

Language skills

Although not always directly related to eikaiwa teaching as some eikaiwa schools may operate an English-only policy for its teachers, Peter, Roger, and Matthew mentioned Japanese language as an important skill they developed as a result of living and working in Japan. Roger, for example, stated that he had studied Japanese at university, but gained a deeper exposure to the language by listening to his eikaiwa manager interact with the parents of the children he taught. Each of the three interviewees now use Japanese daily to communicate with colleagues, clients, and customers.

Research skills

Another indirect skill that may be gained from eikaiwa teaching is research. For example, Hooper & Snyder (2017) describe the journey of an eikaiwa teacher embarking on a part-time master's degree program and engaging in research to work on his professional development. I also began to develop my research skills while at eikaiwa and investigated aspects of my classroom teaching for my own master's study (See p. 161). Roger stated that his eikaiwa experience helped lead him to post-graduate study and employment in tertiary education which in turn enhanced his research skills – "*my skills have come from working in education, particularly tertiary education and having to do my own research*." Now, as a project development manager, he utilises these skills to research market trends, compile information, and report it to his team and manager. He argues that his ability to research developed through his career in teaching that began at an eikaiwa school.

Conclusion

In this chapter, I have described the various skills that ten interviewees deemed as transferable to and useful in their subsequent or current professions after leaving eikaiwa. It thereby offers a more positive account of the eikaiwa experience by illustrating how an eikaiwa teaching position has benefited individuals in terms of their development as working professionals as they have moved on to alternative careers. Although more research is needed with a wider sample of participants to make any solid claims about the benefits of beginning one's career at an eikaiwa, the ten interviewees could all identify skills that they developed while language teaching that have been of subsequent value to them. Also, it is interesting to note that three of the interviewees (Paul, Miyuki, & James) returned to language teaching in Japan after initially leaving the field. Thus, one can argue that eikaiwa provides an important grounding in language teaching that may then become a useful fall-back career for people if circumstances dictate it. Eikaiwa teaching may not be for everybody. However, it may provide some with an exciting and worthwhile entry into the world of work and life thereafter.

16. What can we learn from eikaiwa? Unveiling a complex and evolving entity

Daniel Hooper
Natasha Hashimoto

The origins of this project came, at least in part, from our meeting in 2017 at a conference in central Japan where we initially became aware of each other's interest in eikaiwa. Although many teachers attending TESOL conferences in Japan started their careers in English conversation schools, there seemed to be only a very small community of people who kept up to date with or actually engaged in research about eikaiwa. Therefore, we naturally tended to gravitate towards the other familiar "eikaiwa people" that we stumbled upon from time to time. Recognising each other as fellow "eikaiwa people," we resolved to stay in contact via email. Over the months that passed, we both discussed our time as eikaiwa teachers as well as our research and critical perspectives related to our experiences. We slowly unpacked certain issues related to eikaiwa such as pedagogical constraints and affordances, teacher development, and race and gender, while considering the rich, multi-layered stories and interpretations that we were exposed to through conversing with our growing network of former and current eikaiwa teachers.

It became clear that there was much of the eikaiwa experience that was insufficiently explored in the existing research on English conversation schools in Japan. Furthermore, we felt that these conversation schools were viewed by many teachers in international schools or universities as an inconvenient truth, a simplistically-framed context that they preferred to stigmatise or just forget about completely. Rather than pigeonholing eikaiwa schools (and teachers) into a convenient representation of much of what is wrong with Japanese ELT, in this book we have attempted to unveil the complex and evolving reality of what eikaiwa is and who the teachers and students are who engage in it. We have also explored how close (perhaps uncomfortably so for some) it is actually situated to other sectors of Japanese English education. In this final chapter, we will summarise some themes that we draw from the fourteen diverse perspectives presented in this book and what implications they may have for both eikaiwa and the wider field of English teaching in Japan.

Stereotypes and assumptions about eikaiwa

One key theme that emerged throughout this volume was the problematisation of several enduring and prevalent stereotypes associated with eikaiwa schools. As we will illustrate in this section, "common-sense" assumptions about eikaiwa schools were challenged in this book in two ways: 1) we questioned the notion of eikaiwa as one uniform entity, and 2) highlighted the fact that issues associated with eikaiwa exist in every sector of Japanese ELT.

Partly as a consequence of the "McDonaldization" (Ritzer, 2000) associated with several large chain schools, eikaiwa has commonly been saddled with the image of "McEnglish" - the fast food of language education served by "pedagogical burger-flippers" (McNeill, 2004). This pejorative image of the industry has also been seized upon in expatriate and academic discourse with the image of the "Charisma Man" (Rodney & Garscadden, 2002) - the archetypal male, Caucasian eikaiwa teacher working in a dead-end job and lacking in both integrity and a professional skill set. Unfortunately, these less-than-flattering portrayals of eikaiwa have perhaps been allowed to continue by a marked lack of academic literature on the context (Lowe, 2015). The few studies that do exist have tended to focus on English conversation schools in Japan as "socio-cultural curiosities" (Makino, 2016, p. 4) where white "native-speaker" teachers are fetishised and commodified (Bailey, 2007; Kubota, 2011a). Although these studies have merit in raising critical issues concerning the industry, they may have inadvertently pushed the complexity of eikaiwa classroom practice into the background. Thus, a number of different factors from both inside and outside of ELT have contributed to the prevailing blanket negative attitudes towards eikaiwa schools and those who work in them.

Far from a picture of homogeneity, many chapters in this book describe eikaiwa to be diverse and at times hard to pin down (see chapters in this volume by Iida, Ito, Kiernan, MacDonald, Maschio, Cater). In chapter 8, for example, Maschio illustrates the problematic nature of many accounts utilising eikaiwa as a catch-all term, tending to portray the industry, and in particular its darker traits, as uniform. He argues that the industry is far more dynamic and fluid than previous accounts have suggested and lays out the ways in which it has evolved from the days of the "Charisma Man." A further blanket criticism of eikaiwa related to the charges of "McDonaldization" found in McNeill's (2004) scathing article is the notion of education taking a backseat to business interests. Ito's chapter (chapter 6) provides a powerful counter narrative to this indictment as we are party to the complex negotiation she is engaged in while satisfying the demands of various stakeholders and clients in her business while ensuring she remains true to her strongly ingrained educational and moral principles. Ito's insights on reconciling the push and pull of business and educational demands investigation into the narrative of eikaiwa schools simply "selling out" their principles that has been so uncritically applied up to this point.

Another theme that emerged from this project was the extent to which issues and problems commonly associated with eikaiwa are relevant in many ways to other more formal ELT contexts in Japan (see the chapters by Cater, Hooper, Lawrence, Nuske). In chapter 3, Hooper argues that the eikaiwa industry can be viewed as a "microcosm of Japanese ELT" in that many of the problematic issues that exist in their distilled form in eikaiwa such as discrimination, commercialisation or threats to professional identity represent broader trends in Japanese ELT as a whole. In addition, just as in secondary and tertiary educational contexts, he claims that eikaiwa teachers possess the ability to resist social and institutional forces and use their agency to craft an identity they are satisfied with. This challenges the assumption that eikaiwa teachers are "ideological dupes" (Pennycook, 2001, p. 120) unable or unwilling to question and resist the unreasonable practices and beliefs they are faced with in their workplaces. Jones' reflections (chapter 11) on his professional development within a chain eikaiwa school further highlight the importance of recognising teachers' individual agency when discussing every teaching context, be it formal or informal. Despite few official resources or provisions for teacher development, Jones illustrates how he sought out and took advantage of the opportunities for reflecting on and refining his teaching practice within an informal network of teachers. His story, therefore, draws attention to the problematic nature of eikaiwa teachers being stereotyped as mere cogs in a "McDonaldized" machine and ascribed an identity of passivity and complicity in the face of institutional constraints. In his narrative on the role of formal and informal training in his development as a teacher, Lawrence (chapter 12) also described a feeling that we too have experienced and have seen in others who have moved from eikaiwa teaching into tertiary education.

> ...I was very keen to emphasise my academic credentials and distance myself from the 'unqualified losers' I had left 'behind' in eikaiwa. I was sure that universities were the places where the 'real' teaching and learning happened… (p. 136)

The mindset of believing eikaiwa to be the realm of "unqualified losers" contributes to the position eikaiwa finds itself in the wider field of Japanese ELT today – "a black cloud" on teachers' resumés (Hooper, 2018) that, once they enter the "holy grail" of university teaching (Nagatomo, 2016), they would prefer to forget about. Lawrence illustrates how he came to realise that the stereotype of eikaiwa teaching being devoid of sound professional development was simply a myth. It was the intensely complex and learner-dependent nature of eikaiwa that shaped his journey as an educator. Lawrence's experience shows us that rather than attempting to discount one's eikaiwa teaching past, by recognising without prejudice the tools the context gives teachers, we may achieve a deeper understanding of ourselves and what we can offer our students.

Complexity in eikaiwa

A subscription to a simplistic framing of eikaiwa as "McEnglish" denies the myriad of intersecting contextual and sociocultural factors that influence what happens in these "forgotten" classrooms. Every chapter in this book represents a challenge to the established "McEnglish" narrative by highlighting the multilayered nature of eikaiwa teaching. In this section, we illustrate the complexity that exists in humble eikaiwa schools and is represented in teachers' professional roles, skill sets, identities, and pedagogical approaches.

In chapter 7, based on her autobiographical experience and the narratives of three other former conversation school teachers, Yarwood presents eikaiwa teaching as a negotiation of several different (and sometimes competing) professional roles. Yarwood argues that eikaiwa teachers often juggle the multiple identities of service provider, language teacher, psychologist, and motivational coach. This all occurs where teachers are interacting not just with "students" in the traditional sense (where the holder of knowledge has authority), but also with "clients" who hold a substantial power over teachers because eikaiwa schools are commercial enterprises. The power students have as paying clients is in turn backed by the school/company. The teachers in her chapter at times experienced significant emotional stress stemming from the need to frequently switch between expected roles while constantly being at the whim of paying clients. In summary, this chapter reveals an intricate web of power relationships, socioeconomic pressures and conflicting roles that can impact eikaiwa teachers' emotional and mental wellbeing.

Linked to the multitude of roles that eikaiwa teachers may be asked to fulfil is the development of a versatile and diverse professional skill set that can be applicable to the world outside of language teaching. Boon (chapter 15), focuses on the positive skillsets eikaiwa can cultivate by examining the narratives of former eikaiwa teachers. In opposition to the image of eikaiwa as unskilled work, the interviewees, now employed in a wide variety of different professional sectors, stated that they were able to develop their proficiency in several areas such as time management, communication, mentoring, sales, and research in their time as teachers. Taking into account how these former eikaiwa teachers took the skills they had gained from their experiences, we must question the validity of the claim that eikaiwa instruction is essentially "pedagogical burger flipping" (McNeill, 2004).

The two teacher narratives analysed by Kiernan in chapter 13 also serve to further disrupt the pejorative simplification of the eikaiwa experience. As Kiernan states, eikaiwa and professional identity have been regarded as mutually exclusive. This is particularly true when referring to the chain eikaiwa schools, the primary (and often justified) target for accusations of "McDonaldization" due to the "one-size-fits-all" model commonly in place in these institutions and the lack of autonomy that many teachers struggle with as a result. What the narratives in Kiernan's chapter reveal, however, is that eikaiwa teachers are not entirely servants to these top-down pressures and constraints. Stemming from their own unique and multifaceted experiences, beliefs, and ideas of success, both Helen and Graham were able to use negotiation or resistance to craft what they saw as a legitimate professional identity. While Helen created space and authority through advancement in her company, Graham challenged the prescribed practices of the chain eikaiwa he worked at through resistance and subversion. In chapter 10, we also witness MacDonald negotiating his teaching identity and practice in similarly challenging circumstances, working within a strictly administered top-down management structure while attempting to adapt to the starkly different organisational cultures of eikaiwa and *juku*. When faced with a clash between school policy and pedagogical knowledge gained from his MA TESOL course, he surreptitiously implemented a variety of small pedagogical changes that he believed would stimulate greater learning opportunities for his students. While superficially toeing the company line, MacDonald's emerging identity as a language teaching professional led him to seek out spaces for resistance within a commercial model he perceived to be, to a certain extent, detrimental to his students' development. Through the teachers' resistance to institutional constraints shown in Kiernan's and MacDonald's chapters, we are reminded that the experiences and identities of even chain eikaiwa teachers are not simple cause-and-effect relationships where teachers are led like obedient sheep into certain roles by company mandates. Instead, a far more complex negotiation may exist where both institution and individual actively strategise and strive to develop their own interests and desired identities.

One more particularly powerful example of the complexity lying beneath the surface of the eikaiwa classroom can be found in Iida's story of her teaching journey before and after graduate school (chapter 9). Drawing on numerous theories of SLA and insights from educational research, she describes how she gradually came to reevaluate and reinvent her instructional approach and teaching role so as to better empower her students and help them develop into successful English users. Iida's chapter presents readers with a fuller picture of the complex web of considerations that can lie behind eikaiwa teachers' rationale for effective classroom practice. Furthermore, just as in Ito's and Yarwood's chapters (chapters 6 and 7), these decisions need to be negotiated in relation to the external expectations of eikaiwa from parents, students, and society at large. In terms of our original rationale for this book, Iida's and Ito's accounts of their teaching journeys are important. While the caricatures of "Charisma Man" or the "teach-by-numbers" chain eikaiwa teacher do indeed have some basis in reality, we started this project partly because we believe that a sweeping reliance on these easy, negative stereotypes disempowers and trivialises conscientious teachers like Iida and Ito. Assumptions that eikaiwa is simple, monolithic, and trivial act as a self-fulfilling prophecy. They frame these schools as a lost cause and ensure that the very real, problematic issues still existent in the industry stay unaddressed.

Unresolved issues and the road ahead

It is true that many chapters in this book also point to several unresolved and enduring issues in (although not limited to) the eikaiwa industry. Many chapters discussed similar problematic issues even when the negative aspects of the industry were not the sole focus of the chapter. Specifically, the issues of eroding working conditions, deprofessionalisation, lack of adequate support and professional development, and essentialising (as well as the racism and native-speakerism that stem from it) continue to pose a threat to eikaiwa teachers' wellbeing in a variety of contexts. However, these problems are not unique to the eikaiwa sector and are found in ELT at large. Nonetheless, some sections of the eikaiwa sector seem to be rife with the aforementioned problems.

One of the enduring problems that permeates eikaiwa workplaces is that heavy demands are placed on teachers to play a variety of complex roles. These demands are not only taxing but they can have a detrimental impact on teachers. To illustrate, a language teacher might have to be a language teacher, entertainer, consultant, sales rep, and psychologist to students (further examples are provided in Hashimoto, Hooper, Jones, MacDonald, Nuske, and Yarwood, this volume). Research indicates that emotional labour demands (Hochschild, 1983) have a damaging effect on teacher populations globally (Tsang, 2018). Emotional labour and its consequences are an important issue and more attention needs to be paid to this aspect of the eikaiwa industry because emotional labour takes its toll on eikaiwa teachers as well (see, in particular, the chapters written by Jones, MacDonald, and Yarwood, for detailed accounts of emotional labour and cognitive burden placed upon the teachers).

In addition, the issue of teacher proofing (minimised or lacking teachers' control over curricula, Eryaman & Riedler, 2010) can, in some instances, lead to deskilling of the profession, which is elaborated on in the chapters authored by Hashimoto, Kiernan, Maschio, Nuske, and Yarwood. Although what is infamously known as "teacher-proof" curricula and highly prescriptive lesson plans can be helpful in the case of neophyte teachers (explored in Nuske's narrative in this book), in some other instances teacher proofing is demotivating and corrupts teacher professionalism. As Julia, a participant in Yarwood's study (chapter 7), argues, "teachers are the vessels for the method that company is using" (p. 87). It seems, therefore, that teacher proofing continues to be problematic in many schools, particularly large chain eikaiwas.

This controlling of teachers can further extend to schools implementing strict rules that go as far as to dictate what phrases teachers should or should not use. A teacher called Kate reported, in chapter 4, that she and her colleagues were not allowed to use words such "grammar" or "read this," so as not to "scare" learners (p. 54). Moreover, certain conversation topics are censored and a list of acceptable topics are provided for the teachers in Kate's large eikaiwa chain school. Teachers are also required to check the client's file and memorise their listed preferences and "taboos" not to be mentioned before going to the classroom (Yarwood). To enforce these prescribed practices, some schools might install audio monitoring devices in classrooms (Hashimoto, p. 54). Furthermore, some eikaiwa classrooms are glass cubicles (a good example is the Panopticon-like classroom outlay described in Jones' chapter) which ensure easy observation of teachers' behaviour. Combined with sometimes uncomfortable and even unsafe working environments (Yarwood) and low pay (Kiernan), the overwhelming cognitive and emotional demands that some eikaiwa teachers have to deal with may cause teacher burnout, resignation, and poor work performance, through no fault of their own.

Although teacher proofing is extremely constrictive in some instances, the complete opposite, which is a lack of training and professional development, can be equally problematic, as elaborated in Jones', MacDonald's, Nuske's, and Yarwood's chapters, in particular when (novice and uninterested) teachers are simply hired because of their "nativeness" or likeability. When teachers are completely left to their own devices and "the onus [is] placed on [them] to plan everything" (MacDonald, p. 113, this volume), the impression is that the employer thinks of nothing but making a profit. Dedicated teachers have no choice but to try to learn from one another and seek advice from more experienced peers (e.g., described in Jones, Maschio, Nuske).

Despite a lack of training and support from some employers, some teachers are driven to improve and to build an ELT career. After an initial struggle, they grow to appreciate the level of autonomy their schools give them and become good educators, as can be seen in

Boon's, Lawrence's, and MacDonald's narratives. Boon, for example, shares that his eikaiwa work experience served as "an ideal introduction to language teaching" and that he benefited from "the autonomy to develop [his] own lessons and materials" (p. 161). Likewise, as Lawrence suggests, in some instances "context-dependent in-house training and job experience can often provide more practical and effective teaching skills than official qualifications" (p. 132). The potential for eikaiwa to shape professional identities is also illustrated in Nuske's autoethnographic narrative (chapter 14) of an initially unprepared teacher who ventures into the eikaiwa industry by "sheer random chance" (p. 151). Once there, he encounters institutional constraints and native-speakerist ideology in his new workplace. Although he is critical of many eikaiwa practices, Nuske acknowledges the strong influence that the two years that he spent working in the eikaiwa industry have had on forming him as an ELT practitioner. That experience still affects Nuske's "current critical teaching approaches" in his university classroom (p. 158). So, what is the problem? Teachers might have insufficient power to obtain support from their workplaces and their needs might not be fulfilled at all. It is up to employers to provide effective training, and opportunities for professional development, balanced with an appropriate level of teacher autonomy, as the eikaiwa sector is highly unregulated and often lacks internal oversight, too.

Yet another enduring problematic issue in the industry is the essentialising of teachers and learners, based on their culture, gender, nationality, race, and speakerhood status (for detailed accounts, see, in particular, Cater, Lowe, and Nuske). As many eikaiwa teachers are immigrants to Japan, their foreign resident status and original culture can be reasons for their marginalisation in the local community. This was shown in an incident (described by Ito, p. 78), where a parent labelled a long-term Japan resident as a foreigner with no understanding of "Japanese ways". This is a textbook example of essentialising of the Other. It not only reduces the teacher's identity to a static "foreign" one but it challenges the teacher's professional expertise. Similar reductionist stereotyping also manifests in native-speakerism, as discussed in Cater, Hashimoto, Lowe, Nuske, and Yarwood. In chapter 2, Lowe examines several critical incidents from his professional life and, through the vignettes he shares, explains how a variety of native-speaker framings coexisted, or clashed at times, in the eikaiwa schools he worked for. In his narrative, Lowe critically examines interactions with his former eikaiwa colleagues and students. He uncovers how native speaker normativity permeated the schools and was perceived as common sense by many of the actors involved (students, teachers, and supervisors). He points to a variety of ways in which native-speakerism operates in ELT, informing decisions of not only who should teach but also how and what should be taught. NNESTs are often paid less than NESTs (their degree of "nativeness" being the only reason for such a discrepancy in income) and few, even amongst the most qualified NNESTs, succeed in finding full-time eikaiwa work and being accepted by learners and employers (Hashimoto, Yarwood).

Similarly, Hashimoto's participants' narratives (chapter 4) offer a rare insight into how native-speakerism affects foreign NNESTs, as such teachers are typically overlooked by ELT research in Japan. Foreign NNESTs are hired in eikaiwa in limited numbers if they possess desired marketable assets. Ironically, "marketable assets" sometimes include teachers' Whiteness and "native-like" accents in English. The unequal power prevails in the industry: NNESTs are mainly evaluated on how closely they resemble the imaginary ideal NEST. Gatekeepers, most frequently NES interviewers, continue to be the ones who assess how suitable the NNES candidates are for the job. In his narrative, Cater (chapter 5) focuses on a different aspect of native-speakerism and essentialism and his participants are adult eikaiwa learners. More specifically, Cater describes what he learned from his experience of over 10 years of work at a large eikaiwa school, but he also discusses the findings from his earlier studies in the eikaiwa industry. He problematises assumptions and perceptions held by a group of Japanese ELLs about what it means to be authentic as either a NES or Japanese. These categories tend to be juxtaposed and seen as mutually exclusive. One category seems to reinforce the other, allowing this parallel native-speakerism to thrive. Likewise, essentialising means that NESTs can be both privileged and marginalised in the same context (Hooper, Lowe, Nuske).

Overall, poor working conditions and exploitative practices that are present in some eikaiwa schools happen most frequently because of how the management runs the school. When managers have little knowledge about pedagogy and language learning, they are unable to give much needed advice or appraise their teachers properly (Jones, MacDonald, Maschio, and Yarwood). Some school managers might be more concerned about what is beneficial for business, which may result in less favourable conditions for eikaiwa students (Hashimoto, Ito, Kiernan, & Maschio).

Despite the negative aspects of the industry, there is some cause for hope that the eikaiwa sector will evolve positively. We are witnessing an evolution in the industry, and some indication of the start of the current process can be found in several chapters in this book (namely, in Cater, Hashimoto, Iida, Ito, and Maschio). We believe there is evidence that eikaiwa can stand as a locus for, albeit sometimes limited, legitimate professional pedagogy (in particular observable in Iida's and Ito's chapters). Although there is still a long way to go, the narratives included in the present volume challenge the ingrained ideas about what the eikaiwa industry is.

What next?

When we, the editors, read through all the final drafts and discussed what the next step could be as well as how to phrase the final paragraphs of the conclusion, we both uttered sentences with the phrase "we need more…". We have been aware from the start that one of the biggest limitations of the present volume is its lack of POC, female, and nonnative English-speaking authors' voices. We tried to be inclusive when we sent out our call for papers. We wanted a variety of contributors. Unfortunately, in spite of our efforts, we were unable to secure a group of authors as diverse as we had initially planned and hoped for. One reason for this is likely due to the gender imbalance found in EFL teaching in Japanese higher education (Appleby, 2014a; Huang, 2017; Nagatomo, 2016). Because we were aiming for a scholarly but accessible book, we sought out contributors that had a grounding in TESOL/SLA literature. This meant that we were not able to include as many current eikaiwa teachers as we would have liked. Furthermore, while the numbers of former male and female eikaiwa teachers who have crossed over into university teaching may be large, their research interests may not lie along the lines of eikaiwa, but something else. Once they enter higher education, these teachers may prefer to "forget" their eikaiwa days existed.

Thus, we believe that in order to contribute to less stigmatised views of the eikaiwa industry, more academic research on the industry, its practices, and the lived experiences of teachers and learners is needed. It would be particularly valuable to see more research done by insiders: current eikaiwa teachers, managers, owners, and learners. Expanded and continuous investigation of the complexity and peculiarity of the eikaiwa sector might in turn stimulate current teachers to reflect and exercise their agency more and improve their practice. This process can then also raise learners' awareness of how things can be, and thus generates a virtuous cycle of improved conditions for teachers and students alike. It is our hope that at least some of the future research takes up from where this volume ends.

References

Adams, T. E., Jones, S. H., & Ellis, C. (2015). *Autoethnography*. Oxford, UK: Oxford University Press.

Amirian, S. M. R., & Sadeghi, F. (2012). The effect of grammar consciousness-raising tasks on EFL learners performance. *International Journal of Linguistics*, *4*(3), 708-720. doi:10.5296/ijl.v4i3.2392

Anderson, J. (2016). Initial teacher training courses and non-native speaker teachers. *ELT Journal*, *70*(3), 261-274. doi:10.1093/elt/ccv072

Appleby, R. (2013). Desire in translation: White masculinity and TESOL. *TESOL Quarterly*, *47*(1), 122-147. doi:10.1002/tesq.51

Appleby, R. (2014a). *Men and masculinities in global English language teaching*. Basingstoke, UK: Palgrave Macmillan.

Appleby, R. (2014b). White Western male teachers constructing academic identities in Japanese higher education. *Gender and Education, 26*(7), 776-793. doi:10.1080/09540253.2014.968530

Aspinall, R. W. (2012). *International education policy in Japan in an age of globalisation and risk*. Leiden, NL: Global Oriental. doi:10.1163/9789004243729

Bailey, K. (2006). Marketing the eikaiwa wonderland: Ideology, akogare, and gender alterity in English conversation school advertising in Japan. *Environment and Planning D: Society and Space*, *24*(1), 105-130. doi:10.1068/d418

Bailey, K. (2007). Akogare, ideology, and 'charisma man' mythology: Reflections on ethnographic research in English language schools in Japan. *Gender, Place & Culture*, *14*(5), 585-608. doi:10.1080/09663690701562438

Bandura, A. (1997). *Self-efficacy: The exercise of control.* New York, NY: W. H. Freeman and Co.

Barkhuizen, G. (Ed.) (2013). *Narrative research in applied linguistics.* Cambridge, UK: Cambridge University Press.

Barkhuizen, G. (Ed.) (2017). *Reflections on language teacher identity research.* New York, NY: Routledge.

Barkhuizen, G., Benson, P., & Chik, A. (2014). *Narrative inquiry in language teaching and learning research.* New York, NY: Routledge.

Bartolome, A. (2017, September 23). Business mentor: The important role that a mentor plays in the workplace. *ABS-CBN News.* Retrieved from https://news.abs-cbn.com/business/09/23/17/business-mentor-the-important-role-that-a-mentor-plays-in-the-workplace

Befu, H. (2001). *Hegemony of homogeneity.* Melbourne, Australia: Trans Pacific Press.

Benson, P. (2011). *Teaching and researching autonomy* (2nd ed.). Harlow, UK: Pearson.

Boon, A. (2013). Bartender: How would a bartender create a safe, social, and supportive classroom environment? In C. Stillwell (Ed.), *Language teaching from other fields: Sports, arts, and design* (pp. 11-21). Alexandria, VA: TESOL.

Bossaer, A. (2003). The power of perceptions: A look at professionalism in private language schools in Japan. *JALT Hokkaido Journal, 7*, 13-23.

Bourdieu, P. (1986). The forms of capital. In J. Richardson (Ed.), *Handbook of theory and research for the sociology of education* (pp. 241-258). New York, NY: Greenwood.

Braine, G. (2010). *Nonnative speaker English teachers: Research, pedagogy, and professional growth.* New York, NY: Routledge.

Bray, M. (2007). *The shadow education system: Private tutoring and its implications for planners.* Retrieved from http://unesdoc.unesco.org/images/0011/001184/118486e.pdf

Breaden, J. (2016). Education and training for the intercultural competence of Japanese university graduates: Policy, practice, and markets in informal education. In K. Okano (Ed.),

Nonformal education and civil society in Japan (pp. 133- 154). Abingdon, UK: Routledge.

Britton, L. (1992). *Montessori play & learn.* New York, NY: Crown Publishers.

Brotherstone, C. (2014). *Lifer: How to be a bald middle-aged English conversation teacher in Japan* [Kindle edition]. Retrieved from amazon.co.jp

Brown, P. S. (2005). *Elements of learner training and learning strategies in a Japanese eikaiwa (private language school).* Unpublished assignment. Center for English Language Studies, University of Birmingham, Birmingham, UK. Retrieved from https://www.birmingham.ac.uk/Documents/college-artslaw/cels/essays/secondlanguage/Brown1.pdf

Bueno, E. P., & Caesar, T. (Eds.). (2003). *I wouldn't want anybody to know: Native English teaching in Japan.* Tokyo, Japan: JPGS Press.

Burrows, C. (2007). The effect of limited-term contracts on teaching standards at tertiary-level education in Japan. *OnCUE Journal, 1*(1), 64-73.

Caesar, T., & Bueno, E. P. (2003). Introduction. In E. P. Bueno & T. Caesar (Eds.), *I wouldn't want anybody to know: Native English teaching in Japan* (pp. 14-27). Tokyo, Japan: JPGS Press.

Cameron, L. (2001). *Teaching languages to young learners.* Cambridge, UK: Cambridge University Press.

Canagarajah, A. S. (1993). Critical ethnography of a Sri Lankan classroom: Ambiguities in student opposition to reproduction through ESOL. *TESOL Quarterly, 27*(4), 601-626. doi:10.2307/3587398

Carr, W., & Kemmis, S. (1986). *Becoming critical: Education knowledge and action research.* London, UK: Routledge.

Cater, M. A. (2014). *Accept, admit,* and *recognise* in use: A pedagogical corpus study. In N. Sonda & A. Krause (Eds.), *JALT2013 Conference Proceedings* (pp. 284-296). Tokyo, Japan: JALT.

Cater, M. A. (2017). Learner native-speakerism at the eikaiwa gakkou. In P. Clements, A. Krause, & H. Brown (Eds.), *Transformation in language education* (pp. 1-9). Tokyo, Japan: JALT.

Cater, M. A. (2018). Parallel native-speakerisms? *Eikaiwa* learner perceptions of teachers of Japanese. In P. Clements, A. Krause, & P. Bennett (Eds.), *Language teaching in a global age: Shaping the classroom, shaping the world* (pp. 100-107). Tokyo, Japan: JALT.

Chibi, M. (2018). The role of the ESP practitioner as business English teacher. *International Journal of English Literature and Social Sciences (IJELS)*, *3*(2), 197-203. doi:10.22161/ijels.3.2.12

Chomsky, N. (1965). *Aspects of the theory of syntax*. Cambridge, MA: MIT Press.

Clandinin, D. J., & Connelly, F. M. (2000). *Narrative inquiry: Experience and story in qualitative research*. San Francisco, CA: Wiley.

Crookes, G. (2003). *A practicum in TESOL: Professional development through teaching practice*. Cambridge, UK: Cambridge University Press.

Crystal, D. (2006). English worldwide. In R. Hogg & D. Denison (Eds.), *A history of the English language* (pp. 420-439). Cambridge, UK: Cambridge University Press.

Currie-Robson, C. (2014a, January 22). Teachers tread water in eikaiwa limbo. *The Japan Times*. Retrieved from https://www.japantimes.co.jp/community/2014/01/22/voices/teachers-tread-water-in-eikaiwa-limbo/

Currie-Robson, C. (2014b, September 28). Eikaiwa, deal with sexual harassment of teachers before it's too late. *The Japan Times*. Retrieved from https://www.japantimes.co.jp/community/2014/09/28/issues/eikaiwa-deal-sexual-harassment-teachers-late/

Currie-Robson, C. (2015). *English to go: Inside Japan's English teaching sweatshops*. CreateSpace Independent Publishing Platform.

Currie-Robson, C. (2016, January 6). For Japan's English teachers, rays of hope amid the race to the bottom. *The Japan Times*. Retrieved from https://www.japantimes.co.jp/community/2016/01/06/issues/japans-english-teachers-rays-hope-amid-race-bottom/

Davies, A. (2003). *The native speaker: Myth and reality* (2nd ed.). Clevedon, UK: Multilingual Matters.

Denzin, N. (2013). *Interpretive autoethnography*. London: Sage.

Dierkes, J. (2010). Teaching in the shadow: Operators of small shadow education institutions in Japan. *Asian Pacific Educational Review*, *11*(1), 25-35. doi:10.1007/s12564-009-9059-3

Dörnyei, Z. (2009). The L2 motivational self system. In Z. Dörnyei & E. Ushioda (Eds.), *Motivation, language identity and the L2 self* (pp. 9-42). Bristol, UK: Multilingual Matters.

Duarte, C. (2018, June 28). What teaching taught me about sales. *Forbes Community Voice*. Retrieved from https://www.forbes.com/sites/forbesbusinessdevelopmentcouncil/2018/06/28/what-teaching-taught-me-about-sales/

Duff, P. A., & Uchida, Y. (1997). The negotiation of teachers' sociocultural identities and practices in postsecondary EFL classrooms. *TESOL Quarterly*, *31*(3), 451-486. doi:10.2307/3587834

Eby, L., Rhodes, J., & Allen, T. (2010). Definition and evolution of mentoring. In T. Allen & L. Eby (Eds.), *The Blackwell handbook of mentoring* (pp. 7-20). Malden, MA: Blackwell Publishing.

Eiken Foundation of Japan. (n.d.). *Overview of the EIKEN tests*. Retrieved from https://www.eiken.or.jp/eiken/en/eiken-tests/overview/

Ellis, R. (2005). Principles of instructed language learning. *System*, *33*(2), 209-224. doi:10.1016/j.system.20004.12.006

Ellis, R. (2009). Task-based language teaching: Sorting out the misunderstandings. *International Journal of Applied Linguistics*, *19*(3), 221–246. doi:10.1111/j.1473-4192.2009.00231.x

Ellis, R., & Shintani, N. (2014). *Exploring language pedagogy through second language acquisition research*. London, UK: Routledge.

Entrich, S. (2018). *Shadow education and social inequalities in Japan: Evolving patterns and conceptual implications* [E-Reader Version]. Retrieved from https://library.temple.edu/

Eryaman, M., & Riedler, M. (2010). Teacher-proof curriculum. In C. Kridel (Ed.), *Encyclopedia of curriculum studies* (pp. 865-865). Thousand Oaks, CA: SAGE Publications Inc. doi:10.4135/9781412958806.n457

Falout, J., & Murphey, T. (2018). Teachers crafting job crafting. In S. Mercer & A. Kostoulas (Eds.), *Language Teacher Psychology* (pp. 211-230). Bristol, UK: Multilingual Matters.

Fanselow, J. (2018). *Small changes in teaching big results in learning: Videos, activities and essays to stimulate fresh thinking about language learning.* Tokyo, Japan: iTDi TESOL.

Feagin, J. R. (2013). *The white racial frame: Centuries of racial framing and counter-framing* (2nd ed.). New York, NY: Routledge.

Ford, L. (2004, May 20). 'McJob' status hard to break. *The Guardian.* Retrieved from https://www.theguardian.com/education/2004/may/20/tefl2

Forsyth, P. (2007). *Successful time management* (2nd ed.). London, UK: Kogan Page Ltd.

Foucault, M. (1995). *Discipline and punish: The birth of the prison.* New York, NY: Vintage.

Fukunaga, S., Hashimoto, N., Lowe, R. J., Unser-schutz, G., & Kusaka, L. (2018). Collaborative Deconstruction of Native-Speakerism. In P. Clements, A. Krause, & H. Brown (Eds.), *Language Teaching in a global Age: Shaping the classroom, shaping the world* (pp. 33-42). Tokyo, Japan: JALT

Gaba. (n.d.). *Why Japan?* Retrieved from https://www.gabateachinginjapan.com/locations/kanto/

Gagné, A., Herath, S., & Valencia, M. (2018). Exploring privilege and marginalization in ELT: A trioethnography of three diverse educators. In B. Yazan & N. Rudolph (Eds.), *Criticality, teacher identity, and (in)equity in English language teaching* (Vol. 35, pp.

237–256). Singapore: Springer. doi:10.1007/978-3-319-72920-6_13

GaijinPot. (n.d.). *GaijinPot jobs.* Retrieved from: https://jobs.gaijinpot.com

Galloway, N. (2014). "I get paid for my American accent": The story of one multilingual English teacher (MET) in Japan. *Englishes in Practice*, *1*(1), 1-30. doi:10.2478/eip-2014-0001

Gay, L. (2009, October 1). The McJob of Asia. Japan Today. Retrieved from https://japantoday.com/category/features/opinions/the-mcjob-of-asia

General Union. (n.d.). *Language Schools.* Retrieved from http://www.generalunion.org/language-schools

Gilligan, C. (1982). *In a different voice.* Cambridge, MA: Harvard University Press.

Grandey, A. (2000). Emotional regulation in the workplace: A new way to conceptualize emotional labor. *Journal of Occupational Health Psychology*, *5*(1), 95-110. doi:10.1037//1076-8998.5.1.95

Gray, J., & Block, D. (2013). The marketisation of language teacher education and neoliberalism: characteristics, consequences and future prospects. In D. Block, J, Gray & M. Holborow (Eds.), *Neoliberalism and applied linguistics* (pp. 119-148). London, UK: Routledge.

Griffiths, K, M., Nakane, Y., Chistensen, H., Yoshioka, K., Jorm A, F., & Nakane, H. (2006). Stigma in response to mental disorders: a comparison of Australia and Japan. *BMC Psychiatry*, *6*(21), doi:10.1186/1471-244X-6-21.

Hall, I. P. (1998). *Cartels of the mind: Japan's intellectual closed shop.* New York, NY: W.W. Norton & Co.

Hashimoto, K. (2009). Cultivating "Japanese who can use English": Problems and contradictions in government policy. *Asian Studies Review*, *33*(1), 21-42. doi:10.1080/10357820802716166

Hashimoto, N. (2013a). Analysis of interaction in ELF between Japanese L1 speakers and foreign students of Japanese in a multicultural discussion session. *Temple University Japan Studies in Applied Linguistics, 87*, 23-36.

Hashimoto, N. (2013b, October). *"Much deeper than just English!" – Eikaiwa learners' struggles and aspirations.* Paper presented at the JALT2013 International Conference, Kobe, Japan.

Hashimoto, N. (2014a, September). *Nonnative/bilingual English speaking teachers discuss inequality, teaching anxieties, and perseverance.* Paper presented at the 2nd International Symposium on Native-Speakerism, Saga, Japan.

Hashimoto, N. (2014b, November). *Native English speaking teachers of Asian descent – The eikaiwa experience.* Paper presented at JALT2014 International Conference, Tsukuba, Japan.

Hatta, T., & Kawakami, A. (1995). Patterns of handedness in modern Japanese: a cohort effect shown by re-administration of the HN Handedness Inventory after 20 years. *Canadian Journal of Experimental Psychology/Revue canadienne de psychologie expérimentale, 49*(4), 505-512.

Hattie, J. (2012). *Visible learning for teachers: Maximizing impact on learning.* New York, NY: Routledge.

Hayes, B. E. (2013). Hiring criteria for Japanese university English-teaching faculty. In S. A. Houghton & D. J. Rivers (Eds.), *Native-speakerism in Japan: Intergroup dynamics in foreign language education* (pp. 132-146). Bristol, UK: Multilingual Matters.

Hiramoto, M. (2013). English vs English conversation: Language teaching in modern Japan. In L. Wee, R. B. H. Goh, and L. Lim (Eds.), *The Politics of English: South Asia, Southeast Asia and the Asia Pacific* (pp. 228-248). Amsterdam, Netherlands: John Benjamins.

Holliday, A. (1994). *Appropriate methodology and social context.* Cambridge, UK: Cambridge University Press.

Holliday, A. (2005). *The struggle to teach English as an international language.* Oxford, UK: Oxford University Press.

Holliday, A. (2006). Native-speakerism. *ELT Journal, 60*(4), 385-387. doi:10.1093/elt/ccl030

Holliday, A. (2015). Native-speakerism: Taking the concept forward and achieving cultural belief. In A. Swan, P. Aboshiha, & A. Holliday (Eds.), *(En)Countering native-speakerism: Global perspectives* (pp. 11-25). London, UK: Palgrave Macmillan. doi:10.1057/9781137463500_2

Holliday, A. (2018). *Understanding intercultural communication: Negotiating a grammar of culture* (2nd ed.). Abingdon, UK: Routledge.

Hooper, D. (2017, November). *From "McEnglish" to "the holy grail": Eikaiwa and university through the eyes of educators.* Paper presented at JALT2017 International Conference, Tsukuba, Japan.

Hooper, D. (2018). Too close for comfort: Eikaiwa and stigma in Japanese ELT. *Speakeasy*, *30*, 32-38.

Hooper, D. (2019a). From "McEnglish" to the "holy grail": Transitions between eikaiwa and university teaching. *TESL-EJ, 23*(1). Retrieved from http://www.tesl-ej.org/wordpress/issues/volume23/ej89/ej89a8/

Hooper, D. (2019b). Serious leisure: A diary study of self-directed learning and motivation in eikaiwa. *The Learner Development Journal*, *2,* 20-40.

Hooper, D., Oka, M., & Yamazawa, A. (2020). Not all *eikaiwas* (or instructors) are created equal: A trioethnography of 'native speaker' and 'non-native speaker' perspectives on English conversation schools in Japan. In R. Lowe & L. Lawrence (Eds.), *Duoethnography in English language teaching: Research, reflection, and classroom pedagogy.* Bristol, UK: Multilingual Matters.

Hooper, D., & Snyder, W. (2017). Becoming a "real" teacher: A case study of professional development in eikaiwa. *The European Journal of Applied Linguistics and TEFL*, *6*(2), 183-201.

Houghton, S. A., & Rivers, D. J. (2013). Introduction: Redefining native-speakerism. In S. A. Houghton & D. J. Rivers (Eds.), *Native-speakerism in Japan: Intergroup dynamics in foreign language education* (pp. 1-14). Bristol, UK: Multilingual Matters.

Huang, F. (2017, October). *Who are they and why did they move to Japan? An analysis of international faculty at universities* (Working Paper

No. 27). London, UK: UCL Centre for Global Higher Education. Retrieved from http://www.researchcghe.org/perch/resources/publications/wp27.pdf.

Hutchinson, T., & Waters, A. (1987). *English for specific purposes.* Cambridge, UK: Cambridge University Press.

IIBC (Institute for International Business Communication). (2018). *Presu ririisu: 2017 nendo TOEIC®Program Soujukenshasuu ha yaku 270man nin.* Retrieved from http://www.iibc-global.org/iibc/press/2018/p092.html

Ito, L. (2019). How should grammar be taught to children? *The Language Teacher, 43*(23), 35-37.

iza_kaiser. (2015, February 6). *Do you lie about your job? – The stigma against teaching English in Japan* [Msg 49]. Message posted to https://www.reddit.com/r/japan/comments/2uygp0/do_you_lie_about_your_job_the_stigma_against/

JALT (The Japan Association for Language Teaching). (n.d.). *About us.* Retrieved from https://jalt.org/main/about

Japan Today. (2007, October 26). *Nova granted court protection from creditors; president missing.* Retrieved from https://www.webcitation.org/5SyBTy4Zy?url=http://www.japantoday.com/jp/news/420582

Japan Today. (2015, February 21). *Why is teaching at English conversation schools in Japan such a maligned profession by some people?* Retrieved from https://japantoday.com/category/have-your-say/why-is-teaching-at-english-conversation-schools-in-japan-such-a-maligned-profession-by-some-people-2

Japan Today. (2017, October 7). *Lefties finally getting their due in Japan.* Retrieved from https://japantoday.com/category/features/kuchikomi/lefties-finally-getting-their-due

Jenkins, J. (2007). *English as a lingua franca: Attitude and identity.* Oxford, UK: Oxford University Press.

Kachru, B. B. (1985). Standards, codification, and sociolinguistic realism: The English language in the outer circle. In R. Quirk

& H. Widdowson (Eds.), *English in the world: Teaching and learning the language and literature* (pp. 11-30). Cambridge, UK: Cambridge University Press.

Kachru, B. B. (1990). *The alchemy of English: The spread, functions and models of non-native Englishes.* Urbana, IL: University of Illinois Press.

Katz, L. G. (1997). Child development knowledge and teachers of young children [Monograph]. *ERIC Clearinghouse on Elementary and Early Childhood Education, 217*, 1-79.

Kawai, Y. (2007). Japanese nationalism and the global spread of English: An analysis of Japanese governmental and public discourses on English. *Language and Intercultural Communication, 7*(1), 37-55. doi:10.2167/laic174.0

Kelley, C. E. (2013). *Accidental immigrants and the search for home: Women, cultural identity, and community.* Philadelphia, PA: Temple University Press.

Kelsky, K. (2001). *Women on the verge: Japanese women, Western dreams.* Durham, UK: Duke University Press.

Kiernan, P. (2010). *Narrative identity in English language teaching: Exploring teacher interviews in Japanese and English.* Basingstoke, UK: Palgrave Macmillan.

Kikuchi, D. (2017, March 9). Teachers claim dismissals were invalid in suit against Shane English School. *The Japan Times.* Retrieved from https://www.japantimes.co.jp/news/2017/03/09/national/teachers-claim-dismissals-invalid-suit-shane-english-school/

Kramsch, C. (1998). *Language and culture.* Oxford, UK: Oxford University Press.

Krashen, S. D. (1985). *The input hypothesis: Issues and implications.* New York, NY: Longman.

Kubota, R. (2011a). Learning a foreign language as leisure and consumption: Enjoyment, desire, and the business of eikaiwa. *International Journal of Bilingual Education and Bilingualism, 14*(4), 473-488. doi:10.1080/13670050.2011.573069

Kubota, R. (2011b). Questioning linguistic instrumentalism: English, neoliberalism, and language tests in Japan. *Linguistics and Education*, *22*(3), 248-260. doi:10.1016/j.linged.2011.02.002

Kubota, R. (2016). Neoliberal paradoxes of language learning: Xenophobia and international communication. *Journal of Multilingual and Multicultural Development*, *37*(5), 467-480. doi:10.1080/01434632.2015.1071825

Kubota, R. (2018). *Eigo kyōiku gensō* [Misconceptions of English language teaching and learning]. Tokyo, Japan: Chikuma Shinsho.

Kumaravadivelu, B. (2012). *Language teacher education for a global society: A modular model for knowing, analyzing, recognizing, doing, and seeing*. New York, NY: Routledge.

Lai, M. L. (1999). JET and NET: A comparison of native-speaking English teachers' schemes in Japan and Hong Kong. *Language Culture and Curriculum*, *12*(3), 215-228. doi:10.1080/07908319908666579

Larson-Hall, J. (2008). Weighing the benefits of studying a foreign language at a younger starting age in a minimal input situation. *Second Language Research*, *24*(1), 35-63. doi:10.1177/0267658307082981

Lawrence, L. (2017a). The role of student-led social media use in group dynamics. *The Language Teacher, 41*(5), 17-22.

Lawrence, L. (2017b). Transforming classes through group dynamics: From theory to practice. In P. Clements, A. Krause, and E. Brown (Eds.), *Transformation in language education* (pp. 280-286). Tokyo, Japan: JALT.

Lee, S. I., Murphy-Shigematsu, S., & Befu, H. (2006). *Japan's diversity dilemmas: Ethnicity, citizenship, and education*. New York, NY: iUniverse.

Lewis, M. (1993). *The lexical approach*. Hove, UK: Language Teaching Publications.

Lie, J. (2004). *Multiethnic Japan*. Cambridge, MA: Harvard University Press. doi:10.4159/9780674040175

Linse, C. T., & Nunan, D. (2006). *Practical English language teaching: Young learners.* New York, NY: McGraw-Hill.

Llurda, E. (2015). Non-native teachers and advocacy. In M. Bigelow & J. Ennser-Kananen (Eds.), *The Routledge handbook of educational linguistics* (pp. 105-116). New York, NY: Routledge.

Long, M. H. (1996). The role of the linguistic environment in second language acquisition. In W. C. Ritchie & T. K. Bhatia (Eds.), *Handbook of second language acquisition* (pp. 413-468). New York, NY: Academic Press.

Lowe, R. J. (2015). Cram schools in Japan: The need for research. *The Language Teacher*, *39*(1), 26-31.

Lowe, R. J. (forthcoming). *Uncovering ideology in English language teaching: Identifying the 'native speaker' frame.* Singapore: Springer.

Lowe, R. J., & Kiczkowiak, M. (2016). Native-speakerism and the complexity of personal experience: A duoethnographic study. *Cogent Education*, *3*(1), 1264171. doi:10.1080/2331186X.2016.1264171

Lowe, R. J., & Lawrence, L. (2018). Native-speakerism and 'hidden curricula' in ELT training: A duoethnography. *Journal of Language and Discrimination*, *2*(2), 162-187. doi:10.1558/jld.36409

Lowe, R. J., & Pinner, R. (2016). Finding the connections between native-speakerism and authenticity. *Applied Linguistics Review*, *7*(1), 27-52. doi:10.1515/applirev-2016-0002

Luke, A. (2009). Race and language as capital in school: A sociological template for language-education reform. In R. Kubota & A. M. Y. Lin (Eds.), *Race, culture, and identities in second language education: Exploring critically engaged practice* (pp. 286-308). London, UK: Routledge.

Lummis, D. (1976). *Ideorogi to shite no eikaiwa* [English conversation as ideology]. Tokyo, Japan: Shobunsha.

MacDonald, E. (2017). Ask your students: Japanese students' feelings and beliefs on homework in juku. *Explorations in Teacher Development*, *24*(2), 13-21.

MacDonald, E. (2019). Reflection through dialogue: Conducting a mentoring session with a *juku* colleague using the 'Wheel of Reflection' tool. *Relay Journal*, *2*(1), 45-59.

Makino, M. (2015). Principled eikaiwa. *JALT School Owners SIG Newsletter*, *1*, 3-8.

Makino, M. (2016). A taxonomy of eikaiwa schools. *JALT School Owners SIG Newsletter*, *3*, 4-11.

Martial Reviews. (n.d.). *10 warning signs of a McDojo*. Retrieved from http://www.martialreviews.com/blog/10-warning-signs-of-a-mcdojo

Mascetti, J. (2018, January 20). Facing the 'two-year mark' in Japan: Should I stay or should I go? *The Japan Today*. Retrieved from https://japantoday.com/category/features/lifestyle/facing-the-%E2%80%98two-year-mark%E2%80%99-in-japan-should-i-stay-or-should-i-go

Matsuda, A. (2003). The ownership of English in Japanese secondary schools. *World Englishes*, *22*(4), 483-496. doi:10.1111/j.1467-971X.2003.00314.x

McAdams, D. P., Josselson, R., & Lieblich, A. (2006). *Identity and story: Creating self in narrative*. Washington, DC: American Psychological Association.

McBeath, N. (2017). Initial teacher training courses and non-native speaking teachers: a response to Jason Anderson. *ELT Journal*, *71*(2), 247–249. doi:10.1093/elt/ccw090

McCrostie, J. (2014, June 16). Harassers exploit Gaba's 'man-to-man' lesson format. *The Japan Times*. Retrieved from https://www.japantimes.co.jp/community/2014/06/16/issues/harassers-exploit-gabas-man-man-lesson-format/

McKenzie, M. R., & Gilmore, A. (2017). "The people who are out of 'right' English": Japanese university students' social evaluations of English language diversity and the internationalisation of Japanese higher education. *International Journal of Applied Linguistics*, *27*(1), 152-175. doi:10.1111/ijal.12110

McMansion Hell. (n.d.). *About.* Retrieved from https://mcmansionhell.com/about

McNeill, D. (2004, February 24). McEnglish for the masses. *The Japan Times.* Retrieved from https://www.japantimes.co.jp/community/2004/02/24/issues/mcenglish-for-the-masses/

McVeigh, B. (2004). Foreign language instruction in Japanese higher education: The humanistic vision or nationalistic utilitarianism? *Arts and Humanities in Higher Education, 3*(2), 211-227. doi:10.1177/1474022204042687

Medina, J. (2014). *Brain rules for baby.* Seattle, WA: Pear Press.

Merriam-Webster. (n.d.). *McJob.* Retrieved from https://www.merriam-webster.com/dictionary/McJob#h1

METI (Ministry of Economy, Trade and Industry). (2017). *Preliminary report on the current survey of commerce.* Retrieved from http://www.meti.go.jp/english/statistics/index.html

METI (Ministry of Economy, Trade and Industry). (2019a). *Foreign language conversation schools.* Retrieved from www.meti.go.jp/statistics/tyo/tokusabido/result/result_1/xls/hv15601j.xls

METI (Ministry of Economy, Trade and Industry). (2019b). *2019 statistical survey on specific service industries.* Retrieved from http://www.meti.go.jp/statistics/tyo/tokusabido/result-2.html

MEXT (Ministry of Education, Culture, Sports, Science and Technology). (2014). *English Education Reform Plan corresponding to Globalization.* Retrieved from http://www.mext.go.jp/en/news/topics/detail/__icsFiles/afieldfile/2014/01/23/1343591_1.pdf

Ministry of Education, Culture, Sports, Science and Technology (MEXT). (2017). *Nihonjin no kaigai ryuugaku joukyou.* Retrieved from http://www.mext.go.jp/a_menu/koutou/ryugaku/__icsFiles/afieldfile/2017/12/27/1345878_02.pdf

Ministry of Education, Culture, Sports, Science, and Technology (MEXT). (2018). *Shogakko shidoyoryo kaisetsu gaikokugo-katsudo/gaikokugo-hen.* Tokyo, Japan: Kairyudo Shuppan.

Naganuma, Y., Tachimori, H., Kawakami, N., Takeshima, T., Ono, Y., Uda, H., Hata, Y., Nakane, Y., Nakane, H., Iwata, N., Furukawa, Y., & Kikkawa, Y. (2006). Twelve-month use of mental health services in four areas in Japan: Findings from the World Mental Health Japan survey 2002-2003. *Psychiatry and Clinical Neurosciences, 60,* 240-248.

Nagatomo, D. H. (2012). *Exploring Japanese university English teachers' professional identity.* Bristol, UK: Multilingual Matters.

Nagatomo, D. H. (2013). The advantages and disadvantages faced by housewife English teachers in the cottage industry eikaiwa business. *The Language Teacher, 37*(1), 3-7.

Nagatomo, D. H. (2016). *Identity, gender and teaching English in Japan.* Bristol, UK: Multilingual Matters.

Nation, P. (2000). Learning vocabulary in lexical sets: dangers and guidelines. *TESOL Journal, 9*(2), 6-10. doi:10.1002/j.1949-3533.2000.tb00239.x

Nation, P. (2007). The four strands. *Innovation in Language Learning and Teaching, 1*(1), 1-10. doi:10.2167/illt039.0

Noddings, N. (1984). *Caring: A feminine approach to ethics and moral education.* Berkeley, CA: University of California.

Nonaka, C. (2018). *Transcending self and other through akogare (desire): The English language and the internationalization of higher education in Japan.* Bristol, UK: Multilingual Matters.

Noonan, P., & Erickson, A. G. (2018). *The skills that matter.* Thousand Oaks, CA: Corwin.

Norton, B. (2001). Non-participation, imagined communities and the language classroom. In M. Breen (Ed.), *Learner contributions to language learning: New directions in research* (pp. 159-171). Harlow, UK: Pearson Education.

Nuske, K. (2014). "It is very hard for teachers to make changes to policies that have become so solidified": Teacher resistance at corporate eikaiwa franchises in Japan. *The Asian EFL Journal 16*(2), 283-312.

Nuske, K. (2015). Transformation and stasis: Two case studies of critical teacher education in TESOL. *Critical Inquiry in Language Studies, 12*(4), 283-312. doi:10.1080/15427587.2015.1096734

Nuske, K. (2016). Novice practitioners' views on the applicability of postmethod and critical pedagogy in Saudi EFL contexts. In L. Buckingham (Ed.), *Language, identity and education on the Arabian peninsula: Bilingual policies in a multilingual context* (pp. 119-219). Bristol, UK: Multilingual Matters.

Nuske, K. (2018). "I mean I'm kind of discriminating my own people:" A Chinese TESOL graduate student's shifting perceptions of China English. *TESOL Quarterly*, *52*(2), 360-390. doi:10.1002/tesq.404

Nuske, K. (2019). Vehicle of erotic liberation of instrument of career survival? Japan's ideologies of English as reflected in conversation school advertisements. *Discourse, Context, and Media*, *31*, 1-10. doi:10.1016/j.dcm.2019.100319

Oakland, M. (2010, May 15). Back to the 'eikaiwa' drawing board. *The Japan Times.* Retrieved from https://japantoday.com/category/features/opinions/back-to-the-eikaiwa-drawing-board

Ochs, E., & Capps, L. (2001). *Living narrative: Creating lives in everyday storytelling.* Cambridge, MA: Harvard University Press.

Papageorgiou, I., Copland, F., Viana, V., Bowker, D., & Moran, E. (2019). Teaching practice in UK ELT master's programmes. *ELT Journal*, *73*(2), 154-165. doi:10.1093/elt/ccy050

Pennycook, A. (2001). *Critical applied linguistics: A critical introduction.* Mahwah, NJ: Lawrence Erlbaum.

Perkins, H. C., & Thorns, D. C. (2012). *Place, identity and everyday life in a globalizing world.* Basingstoke, UK: Palgrave.

Petric, B. (2009). 'I thought I was an Easterner; it turns out I am a Westerner!' EIL migrant teacher identities. In F. Sharifian (Ed.), *English as an international language: Perspectives and pedagogical issues* (pp. 135-150). Bristol, UK: Multilingual Matters.

Phillipson, R. (1992). *Linguistic imperialism.* Oxford, UK: Oxford University Press.

Pinter, A. (2006) *Teaching young language learners.* Oxford, UK: Oxford University Press.

Popescu, A. V. (2010). A general view on the relationship between ESP and EGP. *Professional communication and translation studies, 3*(1-2), 49-52. Retrieved from https://www.cls.upt.ro/files/conferinte/proceedings/2010/PCTS_3_2010.pdf#page=56

Pritchard, P. (1987). *The making of McPaper: The inside story of USA TODAY.* Kansas City, MO: Andrews McMeel & Parker.

Riessman, C. K. (2001). Analysis of personal narratives. In J. F. Gubrium & J. A. Holstein (Eds.), *Handbook of interview research: Context and method* (pp. 695-710). Thousand Oaks, CA: Sage.

Reissman, C. K. (2008). *Narrative methods for the human sciences.* Los Angeles, CA: Sage.

Richards, J. C., & Farrell, T. S. C. (2005). *Professional development for language teachers.* Cambridge, UK: Cambridge University Press.

Rivers, D. J. (2013). Implications for identity: Inhabiting the 'native speaker' English teacher location in the Japanese sociocultural context. In D. J. Rivers & S. A. Houghton (Eds.), *Social identities and multiple selves in foreign language education* (pp. 32-55). London, UK: Bloomsbury.

Rodney, L., & Garscadden, N. (2002). *Charisma man: The complete collection.* Tokyo, Japan: AKNG Press.

Rodriguez, E., Shofer, S., Harter, M. & Clark, N. (2017). First guiding process: problematizing what you know for new-self insight. In S. Hughes & J. Pennington (Eds.), *Autoethnography* (pp. 58-87). Thousand Oaks, CA: SAGE Publications, Inc. doi:10.4135/9781483398594

Rosenberg, M. (2013). *Spotlight on learning styles: Teacher strategies for learner success.* Peaslake, UK: Delta Publishing.

Sapunaru-Tamas, C., & Tamas, A. (2012). The eikaiwa phenomenon in Japan or the three-day magic formula: Between marketing and language acquisition. *Osaka Denkitsuushin Daigaku Ningenkagaku Kenkyuu, 14*, 95–106.

Schön, D. A. (1983) *The reflective practitioner: How professionals think in action* [Kindle edition]. New York, NY: Routledge.

Seargeant, P. (2008). Ideologies of English in Japan: The perspective of policy and pedagogy. *Language Policy*, *7*(2), 121-142. doi:10.1007/s10993-007-9079-y

Seargeant, P. (2009). *The idea of English in Japan: Ideology and the evolution of a global language*. Bristol, UK: Multilingual Matters.

Seldin, T. (2006). *How to raise an amazing child the Montessori way*. New York, NY: DK Publishing.

Shearon, B. (2017, June 5). *Changes to the STEP Eiken tests*. Retrieved from http://sendaiben.org/2017/06/05/changes-to-the-step-eiken-tests-june-2017/

Shimizu, A., & Endo, M. (1983). Handedness and familial sinistrality in a Japanese student population. *Cortex*, *19*(2), 265-272. doi:10.1016/S0010-9452(83)80020-3

Simon-Maeda, A. (2004). The complex construction of professional identities: Female EFL educators in Japan speak out. *TESOL Quarterly*, *38*(3), 405-436. doi:10.2307/3588347

Spock, B., & Parker, S. (1998). *Dr. Spock's baby and child care* (7th ed.). New York, NY: Pocket Books.

St. Michel, P. (2015). *Red flags and exit strategies: Advice for English teachers in Japan*. The Japan Times. Retrieved from https://www.japantimes.co.jp/community/2015/10/07/issues/red-flags-exit-strategies-advice-english-teachers-japan/

Stanley, P. (2013). *A critical ethnography of 'Westerners' teaching English in China: Shanghaied in Shanghai*. London, UK: Routledge.

Stebbins, R. A. (2007). *Serious leisure: A perspective for our time*. Edison, NJ: Transaction Publishers.

Stillwell, C. (2013). *Language teaching from other fields: Sports, arts, and design*. Alexandria, VA: TESOL.

Stix, A., & Hrbek, F. (2006). *Teachers as classroom coaches: How to motivate students across the content areas.* Alexandria, VA: ASCD.

Stubbings, B. (2007, September 25). Is it all over for Nova? *The Japan Times.* Retrieved from https://www.japantimes.co.jp/community/2007/09/25/issues/is-it-all-over-for-nova/

Swain, M. (1985). Communicative competence: Some roles of comprehensible input and comprehensible output in its development. In S. M. Gass & C. G. Madden (Eds.), *Input in second language acquisition* (pp. 235-253). Rowley, MA: Newbury House Publishers.

Swain, M. (2005). The output hypothesis: Theory and research. In E. Hinkel (Ed.), *Handbook of research in second language teaching and learning* (pp. 471-483). Mahwah, NJ: Lawrence Erlbaum Associates.

Takahashi, K. (2013). *Language learning, gender and desire: Japanese women on the move.* Tonawanda, NY: Multilingual Matters.

Taylor, J. (2017). Teacher demotivation in a national eikaiwa chain in Japan. In P. Clements, A. Krause, & H. Brown (Eds.), *Transformation in language education* (pp. 62-67). Tokyo, Japan: JALT.

The Japan Exchange and Teaching Programme. (n.d.). Retrieved from http://jetprogramme.org/en/

The Japan Times. (2013, April 14). *Testing children's English ability.* Retrieved from https://www.japantimes.co.jp/opinion/2013/04/14/editorials/testing-childrens-english-ability/

Thornbury, S. (1999). *How to teach grammar.* Harlow, UK: Pearson Education Limited.

Townwork. (2018). *Tokyoto no arubaito, pa-to no heikin jikyuu.* Retrieved from https://townwork.net/tokyo/jikyuu/

Tsang, K. K. (2019). *Teachers' work and emotions: A sociological analysis.* New York, NY: Routledge.

Tsunoda, T. (1978). *Nihon no nou* [The Japanese brain]. Tokyo, Japan: Taishuukan Shoten.

Warren, A. N., & Park, J. (2018). "Legitimate" concerns: A duoethnography of becoming ELT professionals. In B. Yazan & N. Rudolph (Eds.), *Criticality, teacher identity, and (in)equity in English language teaching* (Vol. 35, pp. 199–217). doi:10.1007/978-3-319-72920-6_11

Watson, S., & MacDonald, C. W. E. (2010). English conversation: Oku no hosomichi. *Tohoku Gakuin University College of Liberal Arts Review, 155*, 69-108.

Woods, D. (1996). An integrated view of teachers' beliefs, assumptions and knowledge. In D. Woods (Ed.), *Teacher cognition in language teaching: Beliefs, decision making and classroom practice.* (pp. 184–212). Cambridge, UK: Cambridge University Press.

Yamada, M. (2014). *The role of English teaching in modern Japan: Diversity and multiculturalism through English language education in a globalized era.* New York, NY: Routledge.

Yano Research Institute (2016). *Presu ririsu: Gogaku bijinesu shijou ni kansuru chousa wo jisshi (2016 nen).* Retrieved from https://www.yano.co.jp/press/press.php/001561

Yoder, R. S. (2011). *Deviance and inequality in Japan: Japanese youth and foreign migrants.* Bristol, UK: Policy Press.

Yoshida, K. (2013). Reconsidering Japan's English education based on the principles of plurilingualism. In *Selected papers from the Twenty-second International Symposium on English Teaching* (pp. 121-129). Taipei, Taiwan: Crane.

Zooming Japan. (2013). *All you need to know about working at an eikaiwa in Japan.* Retrieved from: https://zoomingjapan.com/life-in-japan/eikaiwa/

Publication Information

Published by Candlin & Mynard ePublishing Limited,
Unit 1002 Unicorn Trade Centre,
127-131 Des Voeux Road Central,
Hong Kong.

For further information about Candlin & Mynard, please see the website: http://www.candlinandmynard.com

Teacher Narratives From the Eikaiwa Classroom: Moving Beyond "McEnglish"

Life and Education in Japan Series
Series Editors: Diane Hawley Nagatomo and Melodie L. Cook

Published by Candlin & Mynard in ebook and print formats in 2020

Life and Education in Japan Series

Edited by Diane Hawley Nagatomo and Melodie L. Cook

Titles in the series:

Intercultural Families and Education in Japan: Experiences, Issues, and Challenges Edited by Melodie Lorie Cook and Louise George Kittaka

Foreign Female English Teachers in Japanese Higher Education: Narratives From Our Quarter. Edited by Diane Hawley Nagatomo, Kathleen A. Brown, and Melodie L. Cook

Teacher Narratives From the Eikaiwa *Classroom: Moving Beyond "McEnglish."* Edited by Daniel Hooper and Natasha Hashimoto

www.ingramcontent.com/pod-product-compliance
Ingram Content Group UK Ltd.
Pitfield, Milton Keynes, MK11 3LW, UK
UKHW022024190726
13853UKWH00005B/2104